A MANUAL

OF

DISCIPLINE AND INSTRUCTION

For the use of the Teachers of the

PRIMARY AND GRAMMAR SCHOOLS

UNDER THE CHARGE OF THE

Department of Public Instruction

OF THE

CITY OF NEW YORK.

ISSUED BY AUTHORITY OF THE DEPARTMENT.

NEW YORK:
EVENING POST STEAM PRESSES, 41 NASSAU STREET, COR. LIBERTY.

1873.

JOURNAL OF THE BOARD OF PUBLIC INSTRUCTION FOR 1871, PAGE 454.

"*Resolved,* That in order to secure a more thorough and uniform carrying into effect of the various provisions contained in the Course of Instruction for Primary and Grammar Schools, the Committee on Course of Studies, School Books, and Hygienics, cause to be prepared an Expository Manual, containing such recommendations and suggestions as may seem necessary in order to explain more in detail than is practicable in the course itself, the topics which should be taught in each of the prescribed subjects, and the best methods of imparting instruction therein."—*Report of Committee on Course of Studies, &c., Nov. 8th,* 1871.

Signed by

MAGNUS GROSS, Chairman,
HOOPER C. VAN VORST,
TIMOTHY BRENNAN,
} Committee.

Adopted, January 17th, 1872.—*Journal, page* 48.

At a meeting of the Committee on Course of Studies, consisting of Commissioners ISAAC W. ENGLAND, MAGNUS GROSS, and NATHANIEL SANDS, HENRY KIDDLE, City Superintendent, with Assistant-Superintendents T. F. HARRISON and N. A. CALKINS, was authorized to prepare the Manual.

MANUAL

OF

DISCIPLINE AND INSTRUCTION

FOR THE

PRIMARY AND GRAMMAR SCHOOLS.

DUTIES OF THE TEACHER.

No task can be more responsible or require the exercise of greater care than that of educating the young. To perform it aright, special preparation and study are indispensably necessary, not only in relation to the branches of knowledge which may have been selected as a basis for the instruction, but in regard to the proper method and appliances to be employed, in order to render the instruction truly effective. These methods must be determined by a consideration of the faculties to be trained and educated, as well as the nature of the subject taught.

Experience must be, to a great extent, our guide, in enabling us to judge of the character of the minds to be educated, as well as the means employed for carrying on the work.

The teacher's task is one of great magnitude, responsibility, and labor. Great issues depend upon its right performance.

The future welfare of the community depends upon his efforts. Neglect on his part—nay, conscious inefficiency—is a crime. The impressions which are made by him are ineffaceable. Hence it is of supreme importance that his work receive all the guidance that careful study and mature experience can afford.

OBJECT OF THE MANUAL.

The object of this manual is to guide the teachers of the Primary and Grammar Schools in the performance of their duties in relation to both *discipline* and *instruction*.

A careful study of its suggestions will aid them to attain a proper understanding of the requirements of the various grades of the Course of Study, and will enable them efficiently to carry them into effect. It will be the duty of the City Superintendent and his assistants, at every examination of a school, to see that the directions herein contained have been carefully observed by the teachers.

GOVERNMENT AND DISCIPLINE.

GENERAL SUGGESTIONS.

1. In all the rules and methods of discipline employed, the true object of discipline should steadily be kept in view; namely, to train the pupils so that they may form *right habits.*

2. Firmness, vigilance, and uniformity, in dealing with children are of the first importance. The teacher should never resort to violent means, as pushing, pulling, or shaking the children, in order to obtain their attention. All such practices constitute a kind of corporal punishment, and are not only wrong in themselves, but specially prohibited by the Board.

3. Modes of punishment painful to the corporeal system, such

as the sustaining of wearisome burdens, unnatural and long-continued attitudes of restraint, standing, kneeling, &c., are wrongful and injurious. Equally so is the confining of delinquents, by tying them or shutting them in closets. These are all a resort to mere physical force, instead of moral incentives, and involve no appeal to a sense of honor or duty in the child. They do not properly assert the *authority* of the teacher, nor do they really produce *obedience* on the part of the pupil.

4. In directing the various movements required of the pupils, care should be taken never *to touch them.* The teacher should take such a position before the class as will command the eye of every pupil, and thence direct by the voice, or by a signal. Pupils must be habituated to the impression that the teacher will give his commands but *once*, and that they must be obeyed *at once.*

5. *Harsh tones* of the voice are unnecessary and improper. Words of disapprobation may be uttered by the teacher in a tone of *decision*, without the use of any severity that would imply resentment, anger, or antipathy on the part of the teacher. On the contrary, the language used, and the tones of the voice, should always express a feeling of *sympathy* with the child. This is the way to win the youthful mind, and to bend the will, through the affections; a different course will antagonize it, and prevent all real submission, securing only a temporary semblance of obedience.

6. "As is the teacher, so will be the school." It is, therefore, requisite that teachers should rigidly discipline themselves by carefully cultivating habits of neatness, cleanliness, and order, gentleness of manner, a watchful self-control, and a cheerful spirit. In speaking, let the rising inflection of the voice prevail; then, the falling inflection of reproof will be more impressive and effectual.

7. Teachers should seek to obtain the sympathetic regard of the children by giving a due attention to their wants and re-

quests. These should be fulfilled as far as it is proper and reasonable. Children are quick to perceive and to resent injury or injustice. The child who asks for the privilege of a drink of water, for instance, may be suffering acutely ; and, if not accorded relief, when this seems to be perfectly practicable on the part of the teacher, feels a sense of outrage which, for a time, if not permanently, impairs its respect and regard for the teacher. The cultivation of a due feeling of *sympathy* for the children will wholly prevent this. The possession of this feeling in its fulness is the best foundation of success in both discipline and instruction.

8. *Encouragement* inspires confidence, and children, more than others, need it. Let it be given in all cases where this can be honestly done. To a want of this, in the discipline of classes, is to be ascribed the timidity and reserve so often manifested among pupils, by a hesitating manner, a low voice, and a tone of inquiry in response, especially to strangers. A proper degree of encouragement will render them confident and spirited, eager to tell what they know, and in an audible tone of voice. Encouragement has a peculiar influence in promoting mental and moral improvement.

9. *Public exposures and badges of disgrace* belong to a class of punishments which, if ever resorted to, should be employed under careful limitations, and with great circumspection and prudence ; for it requires a skillful, discreet, and conscientious teacher to use them safely and with advantage. In the discipline of girls they should be avoided altogether, as destructive of that nice sense of shame and that delicate sensibility to reputation which should be carefully fostered in the female character.

10. *Cleanliness, method, and regularity* are among the first and most necessary elements of popular education. Every rule requisite to maintain or impart these should be diligently and punctiliously enforced.

11. Education is unfinished while the physical powers are

left untrained. Children should be taught how to sit, to stand, to move, to walk. Rules are required for this; but they need to be but few and simple, and the nice and watchful observation of children renders it quite easy to enforce them, provided they are not capriciously applied. Children must first be taught them, and then *never* permitted to violate them without admonition or correction.

12. Teachers should never forget that their pupils are constantly and closely watching their conduct, and that they are prone to imitate whatever they observe. They should, therefore, see nothing that they may not safely imitate. There is an "unconscious tuition," the silent influence of which produces the most permanent effects.

13. The character of children is greatly affected by their surroundings. These should, therefore, be neat and orderly. The rooms in which they assemble should be clean, the desks and other furniture, as far as possible, without injury or defacement, and everything giving evidence of constant and punctilious attention. Children, from the contemplation of these things, unconsciously acquire habits of order, neatness, and regularity, which have an important bearing upon their usefulness and happiness in after life.

14. The basis of *good order* is attention. It does not require that the pupils should occupy, for any certain time, a fixed position; that they should be compelled to strain their glances upon a given point; that they should be as motionless as statues. All this is unnatural; and whatever is unnatural is really *disorderly*. The postures should be graceful, easy, and uniform, but should be frequently changed; the movements, while as simultaneous as perfect attention would necessarily produce, should also be easy and natural.

COURSE OF INSTRUCTION

PRESCRIBED FOR

PRIMARY SCHOOLS,

WITH

DIRECTIONS AND SUGGESTIONS TO TEACHERS.

SIXTH GRADE.

OUTLINE COURSE.

READING AND SPELLING.—Familiar words, from blackboard and chart; also *spelling* such words from dictation. The printed words to be associated with their meaning by means of conversations with the children.

Elementary Sounds.—Vowels and simple consonants, for training the organs of hearing and speech.

NUMBER.—Counting and adding balls on the numeral frame, by ones to 100, and by twos and threes to 50; also counting other objects.

Arabic Figures.—From 1 to 100, to be read at sight; from 1 to 20 to be written on slates.

OBJECT LESSONS.—*Form.*—Lead the pupils to observe, in various objects, the shape of the square, oblong, cube, ball, cylinder, and then to name these shapes; also, to distinguish the different shapes of corners. The terms straight, crooked, and curved to be taught by their application to objects, lines, etc.

Common objects to be shown and their most obvious parts, shapes, and uses observed by the children.

Color.—The six principal colors, by means of color-cards and other objects.

Human Body and familiar *Animals.*—The principal parts; also the special organs of sense to be pointed out and named.

☞ Each exercise, in object lessons, to be conducted with a view to forming habits of attention and careful observation through the use of the senses.

Drawing and Printing on Slates.—Making dots and small crosses in rows; drawing lines; and printing letters.

N. B.—The exercises of the Sixth Grade should not be continued upon the same subject longer than fifteen minutes at one time.

DIRECTIONS, &c.

Reading.—Teach, first, *short* words that are the *names of familiar* objects.

Special pains should be taken to lead the children to associate the printed words with the objects which they represent, either by the use of the objects themselves, or by pictures.

In teaching words that are not *names*, care should be taken to illustrate their meaning by simple phrases, conversations, etc. During the earlier lessons, omit words of irregular formation, having *several silent letters*, such as *tongue, knife, know, though, thought*, etc. This class of words may be presented when the pupils have learned the alphabet, and its regular combinations have been taught, and some of the sounds represented by the letters.

Let each word be taught first at sight, as a whole, and the sounds and names of the letters which compose the word be taught afterward. After the children have learned a few words at sight, they may be taught the *sounds* and the *letters* which form those words; and, as additional words are learned, the children may be required to name such of the letters as they may know, in the new words, and then taught the remaining ones in those words. In this way the twenty-six letters of the alphabet are to be taught, progressively. Subsequently they are to be reviewed, and their usual order learned by repetition. The *small* letters are, of course, to be taught first.

After the pupils have learned several single words, simple sentences may be presented, as "The dog can bark." "The horse can draw a cart." The other words that make up these sentences can then be learned.

For the purpose of leading the children to observe readily the *analogy of words*, in their sounds and in the arrangement of their letters, after they have learned, objectively and singly, to recognize several words at sight, place on the blackboard, in columns, such of these words as are similar in spelling and in sound, as in the following groups :

cat,	*fan,*	*pin,*	*pen,*	*fox,*	*cup,*
rat,	*man,*	*tin,*	*hen,*	*box,*	*gun,*
hat.	*ran.*	*fin.*	*ten.*	*top.*	*run.*

When the children have learned to pronounce the words in a column, at sight, let them learn to spell each by its sounds, as—*k ă t*, cat; *r ă t*, rat; *h ă t*, hat; etc., not as a *spelling* exercise, but to impress upon their minds the relation of sounds, and letters as their representatives.

Spelling.—After the words have been learned by sight and sound, let them be learned by spelling, and the children requested to observe that similar spelling and similar sounds usually accompany each other.

Of course many words must be taught simply as signs of things, or actions, or qualities, etc., but the plan of grouping words by similarity of sounds will greatly facilitate learning to read.

Various modes may be used in teaching the words singly—for instance : Let the pupil point out given words on the blackboard and on the charts, as they are named by the teacher. A word may be erased from the blackboard, and the pupils requested to pronounce the word, and name the letters composing it. Parts of words may also be erased and the pupils required to name the missing letters.

The list of familiar words taught in this grade should include those commonly used as names of articles of dress, food, furniture, and utensils used in the house, different things used in the school-room, common animals, names of familiar qualities, actions, etc.

It is not the small number of letters of which a word is formed that renders it easy to be learned objectively, but its familiarity by use in conversation. Do not, therefore, confine the pupils to words which are composed of only three or four letters. Long, difficult, or anomalous words should, however, be omitted.

Elementary Sounds.—In first presenting the subject of elementary sounds, the teacher should exemplify, by means of the simple sounds of letters, and require the pupils to repeat by imitation. When their organs of hearing and of speech have thus been trained both to *distinguish* and *imitate* sounds, the teacher may proceed to teach the sounds as represented by letters in simple words.

Among the matters to which teachers should give *special attention*, are the following:

Train the pupils to pronounce words readily at sight.

Do not allow them to use unnatural tones in speaking or reading.

Correct their faults in the use of language as they occur.

NUMBER.—Counting and Figures should be taught at first consecutively in groups or steps, as 0 to 9; 10 to 19; 20 to 29; etc.

The figures should be taught as symbols of the number of objects counted. No succeeding group should be commenced until the preceding one has been thoroughly learned. After the pupils have learned to add balls by *ones*, on the numeral frame, let them add figure *ones*, in single columns, on the blackboard. When they can add balls by *twos*, let them learn to add figure *twos* in single columns.

OBJECT LESSONS.—In teaching *Form*, first present a particular shape by showing an object which represents it; then lead the children to notice and name other objects having the same shape. Let the shape, as a whole, be recognized before the names of its parts are taught.

Color.—The pupils should be led to distinguish and group together like colors, and should learn the names of the six principal colors.

The lessons on *Common Objects* in this grade should be simple, treating only of their most obvious parts, properties, and uses. Such common articles as a bell, chair, slate, pencil, hat, cup, knife, etc., are appropriate for this purpose. The pupils should be led to notice and point out the principal parts, and encouraged to tell what they see and what they know of each object shown them.

In lessons on the *Human Body*, the exercises should lead the pupils to notice and name the parts, as head, neck, trunk, arms, hands, legs, feet; also parts of the head, as crown, face, forehead, cheeks, chin, mouth, nose, eyes, ears, etc.

N. B.—*Each exercise in object lessons should be conducted with a view to forming habits of attention and careful observation through the use of the senses.*

Drawing on Slates, etc.—The exercises of *Drawing* and *Printing on slates* should be introduced in such a manner as to give an interesting variety to the class-work; also, so as to aid in the discipline of the class, by giving the children something *to do* that will interest them after they have become tired with the other lessons. The children might be allowed to use slates for drawing, as a reward for good order and attention. Short daily exercises may be made very useful.

Discipline—The children *should never be compelled to sit without employment for either the mind, the hands, or the body.* They should be taught to be cleanly, to avoid all bad habits, to be truthful and obedient. They should be led to do right by encouragement rather than driven by fear. Judicious praise is more efficient than scolding.

FIFTH GRADE.

OUTLINE COURSE.

READING.—From the blackboard, charts, and Primer. The words to be distinctly pronounced in an easy tone of voice. *The meaning of the words* to be made plain by conversations, and by their use in short familiar phrases or sentences.

Punctuation.—Names and uses of the period and question-mark.

Elementary Sounds.—The pupils to recognize and make the principal vowel sounds in monosyllables; also to make the consonant sounds separately.

Spelling.—Words from the reading lessons; also other familiar words.

NUMBER.—*Counting* and *Adding*, with and without a numeral frame, by threes, fours, and fives to 100; *adding*, separately, the numbers 1, 2, 3, 4, 5, 6, 7, 8, 9, to all numbers below 20; *subtracting* twos, threes, fours, and fives from numbers below 10.

Arabic Figures.—Numbers of three figures (100 to 999) to be read at sight, without numeration; also to be written on slates from dictation.

Roman Numbers.—I, V, and X, with their combinations to XXXIX; pupils to be taught how to tell the time of day from the face of the clock.

OBJECT LESSONS.—Continue the exercises of the Sixth Grade, and in *Form*, lead the pupils to observe, in various objects, the shape of the rhomb, ring, circle, and then to name these shapes; also, to distinguish the wave-line and spiral-line.

Common Objects.—Their obvious parts, uses, and shapes to be distinguished by the pupils.

Color.—The pupils to point out the six principal colors in color-cards, articles of dress, flowers and other objects.

Human Body and familiar *Animals.*—Parts and uses of the limbs; the organs of sense; the names and uses of familiar animals.

DRAWING AND PRINTING ON SLATES.—Connect dots with lines; draw sharp, square, blunt, and round corners; also, lines in given shapes. *Print* words on slates. *Write* small, simple script letters on slates.

N. B.—The exercises of this grade should not be continued, upon the same subject, longer than twenty minutes at one time.

DIRECTIONS, &c.

READING.—In each new lesson in reading in this grade, the first step should be to make the pupils familiar with the words by printing them on the blackboard in columns, and teaching the children to pronounce them at sight. Next, teach them to pronounce at sight the same words in the book, but out of their order in the sentences of the reading lesson. Then teach them to read the lesson *naturally*.

N. B.—*Let the standard for good reading be its near resemblance to good conversation.*

When the lesson has been read, the teacher should talk with the children about it, and encourage them to tell, in their own language, what they have read.

Punctuation.—When printing reading lessons on the blackboard, use the proper punctuation marks, as period and question-mark.

Meaning of Words.—During the lessons of this grade, it is appropriate to teach the children to use the principal words of the lesson in brief sentences, to enable them to show readily that they understand what the words mean, as: "A horse can draw a *cart*."—"I must be *good*."—"I can *hold* a book."—"*Snow* is white."—"I will try to *learn* to read."—"I must *obey* my mother," &c., &c.

Elementary Sounds.—The exercises in sounds should be of such a character as to train the children in distinctness of enunciation both in speaking and reading.

Spelling.—In oral spelling, the words should be distinctly pronounced by the pupil before they are spelled, then each letter clearly uttered, a pause made between the syllables, and the word again pronounced after all the letters have been given. The familiar words taught, in addition to those in the reading lessons, should include such appropriate words as the children most commonly hear and use.

Number.—In counting and adding with the *numeral frame*, do not allow the children to count and add by *rote*. See that due attention is given to the objects counted. When the pupils can add the same number in order, as twos and threes, teach them to add single columns of 2s and 3s on the blackboard, and subsequently on their slates. Let them also learn to add by *twos* and *threes* alternately, naming only the sums thus: 3, 5, 8, 10, 13, 15, 18, 20, 23, 25, etc.

In adding the separate numbers, 1, 2, 3, 4, etc., to numbers below 20, the work should be represented first by balls on the numeral frame and other objects, afterward by figures on the blackboard, thus:

0	1	2	3	4	5	6	7	8	9
1	1	1	1	1	1	1	1	1	1
1	2	3	4	5	6	7	8	9	10

0	1	2	3	4	5	6	7	8	9
2	2	2	2	2	2	2	2	2	2
2	3	4	5	6	7	8	9	10	11

0	1	2	3
3	3	3	3, etc.

When all the numbers from 1 to 9 have been thus presented, and the adding thoroughly taught, a *second step* may be taken, and the numbers from 1 to 9 added to the numbers from 10 to 19 in the same manner.

Writing Arabic Figures.—This can be taught most easily in steps; first, in order, in connection with counting; then, out of order. The following groups will indicate the appropriate steps:

	First Step.	Second Step.	Third Step.	Fourth Step.	Fifth Step.
0...........	10	100	100	200	300
1...........	11	200	101	201	301
2...........	12	300	102	202	302
3...........	13	400	103	203	303
4...........	etc.,	etc.,	etc.,	etc.,	etc.,
5...........	to	to	to	to	to
6...........	99	900	199	299	399
7...........					
8...........					
9...........					

These steps may be continued in this manner through 999. As much time will be required to teach the *first* and *third* steps as for any *four* other steps. Let the children be trained to *read* and *write* the numbers of each step readily before taking up the next one in order.

If properly conducted, these lessons will train the pupils to read and write numbers through 199 in one month, and any number composed of three figures in two months.

Roman Numbers should be so taught in this grade that the children can tell the time of day by the face of a clock.

OBJECT LESSONS.—Most of the suggestions given relative to the *Sixth Grade* for object lessons are equally applicable to those of this grade.

In the lessons on the *human body*, let the pupils point out and give the names and uses of parts, as parts of the arm and hand, legs and feet, joints, etc.

In the lessons on *animals*, let attention be directed chiefly to the domestic animals.

DRAWING, ETC.—The suggestions relative to drawing and printing given for the *Sixth Grade* are also appropriate to this grade.

N. B.—Whenever possible arrange the exercises of each subject so that the pupils may be called upon *to do* something *with their hands*.

Children learn much faster by doing than by merely repeating what they have been told.

FOURTH GRADE.

Outline Course.

Reading—In a First Reader. The articulation to be distinct. The pupils to tell, in their own language, what they have been reading about in the lesson.

Punctuation.—Names of the comma, semi-colon, period, question-mark, and exclamation-mark.

Elementary Sounds.—The sounds of the letters in words of one syllable, to give flexibility to the vocal organs.

Definitions.—The meaning of words to be shown chiefly by their use in phrases or short sentences.

Spelling.—Words from the reading lessons, and other words familiar to children.

Arithmetic.—*Numeration.*—Reading and writing numbers, through. six places (100,000); also, *adding* single columns of ten figures.

Mental Arithmetic.—*Adding,* with and without a numeral frame, by sixes, sevens, eights, nines, and tens to one hundred; also, *subtracting* twos, threes, fours, and fives from numbers below thirty: also, simple practical questions in *addition. Oral Drills* for rapid combinations of two or more numbers, one of which should be less than ten, the other less than one hundred.

Roman Numbers.—I, V, X, L, and C, and their combinations below one hundred.

Object Lessons.—Review the Fifth Grade, and in *Form* lead the pupils to distinguish in various objects, and name the shapes rhomboid, semi-circle, crescent, cone, sphere, and hemisphere; also, the positions of lines, as slanting, vertical, horizontal, and the terms surface and face.

Objects and Qualities.—The principal parts, shape, color, and uses of common objects to be distinguished by the pupils. The terms sticky, slippery, brittle, tough, porous, transparent, opaque, etc., to be illustrated.

Color.—Primary and secondary colors to be distinguished; also, shades and tints, as dark and light colors.

Human Body.—Parts of the arm, hand, foot, head, etc., and their uses.

Animals.—Those used for food; what their flesh is called; wild and tame animals to be designated.

Drawing *and* Slate Writing.—Straight lines to be drawn in various combinations; lines to be divided into equal parts; also, plane figures to be drawn, as squares, oblongs, triangles, rhombs, and rhomboids.

Writing.—Simple words, without capitals, to be written on slates.

N. B.—The exercises of this grade should not be continued, upon the same subject, longer than twenty-five minutes at one time.

FOURTH GRADE.—DIRECTIONS, &c.

READING.—The suggestions relative to teaching *Reading* and *Spelling* in the *Fifth Grade*, are also applicable to instruction in the *Fourth Grade.* Special care should be taken in this grade to train the pupils in habits of clearness and distinctness of enunciation, also to read in an easy, speaking voice. Faults in reading are most readily overcome when the efforts to correct them are chiefly directed to one kind at a time, and the training continued until the pupils clearly perceive the fault and take the proper means to correct it.

Punctuation.—The time commonly spent in teaching children to recite definitions of punctuation marks is wasted. Instead of this, lead the pupils to observe that *a short pause is made at a comma, a little longer pause at a semi-colon,* and still *longer pauses at the question-mark* and *period.* Lead the pupils to see that the question-mark points out a question, and a period the end of a sentence.

Elementary Sounds.—In this grade the pupils should be taught to distinguish the sounds of given letters in words of one syllable, and to make these sounds, as, the sound of *a* in *slate, a* in *ball, o* in *not, o* in *do, u* in *full, f* in *far, f* in *of, k* in *kite, m* in *man, c* in *cow,* etc.

Definitions.—In giving the meaning of words, in some instances, a description of the object, or of its use, if the word be a name, or a simple statement about that which is meant by it, will illustrate the pupils' understanding of it better than the use of the word in a sentence. Let this exercise be so conducted as to avoid mechanical forms of definition, and with a sufficient variety and simplicity to secure a clear knowledge of the *meaning of the words.*

ARITHMETIC.—On commencing *Numeration,* the three places of the units' period should be taught so thoroughly, both on the blackboard and on the slate, that the pupils can name each place at sight—in order and out of order—and can write any number in this period from dictation, before proceeding to teach the period of thousands.

Two or three weeks may be spent thus on the units' period. The pupils should be led to notice the *number* of each place in both the units' and the thousands' period, as first place, second place, fourth place, etc. They should also be led to observe the similarity of names between the first, second, and third places of the units' and the thousands' periods, as units, tens, hundreds of *units*—units, tens, hundreds of *thousands.* Care should be taken to teach the pupils to write the figures plainly and neatly, and in straight columns.

Adding.—Let *adding* be commenced on the blackboard with small numbers and short single columns, as

			4
		2	3
	3	3	2
2	2	2	4
3	2	4	3
—	—	—	—
5	7	11	16

Thus let the numbers be gradually made larger and the columns longer, until the pupils can write upon their slates and add, without counting fingers or other objects, single columns composed of ten figures, all of which shall be 7's, 8's, and 9's.

For drills in *Addition,* in this grade give single columns only.

For drills in *Notation,* give examples of two, three, and four lines, through thousands.—six places.

Oral Drills.—The *oral drills,* in adding, should train the pupils so thoroughly, that they can answer instantly what any number, from one to nine, will make when added to any number below *one hundred.* The exercises for these drills may at first be represented on the blackboard, thus:

2	12	22	32	42	52	62	72	82	92
2	2	2	2	2	2	2	2	2	2
—	—	—	—	—	—	—	—	—	—
4	14	24	34	44	54	64	74	84	94

2	12	22	32	42	52	62	72	82	92
3	3	3	3	3	3	3	3	3	3
—	—	—	—	—	—	—	—	—	—
5	15	25	35	45	55	65	75	85	95

5	15	25	35	45	55	65	75	85	95
4	4	4	4	4	4	4	4	4	4
—	—	—	—	—	—	—	—	—	—

In this way let all the numbers, from 1 to 9, be combined with all the numbers from 2 to 99. The combinations may be erased as fast as the pupils have learned them, and new combinations given. After thus learning them in the order of the decades, let new combinations be formed out of the order of decades, as

5	14	35	44	7	27	76	86
4	5	4	5	6	6	7	7
—	—	—	—	—	—	—	—
9	19	39	49	13	33	83	93

By this means, children can be led to observe that the same numbers always produce a like figure when added, as that 9 and 7 always give the unit 6, whether the numbers be 19 and 7 or 29 and 7, or 37 and 9, or 87 and 9; and thus, by attending to this fact, while adding single columns, they can readily acquire the habit of *adding without counting*, both rapidly and accurately.

Mental Arithmetic.—In the fourth grade the answers to practical questions may be given in the following form: Question—How many are six apples and three apples? Answer—"Six apples and three apples are nine apples." Answer—"Seven cents and five cents are twelve cents."

Object Lessons.—*Form.*—In teaching forms and solids, let the children be led to discover the given shape in other objects than those shown by the teacher. For this purpose frequent reviews should be had without presenting the forms which represent the shapes that have already been learned, when the pupils may be requested to mention several objects of the given shapes.

Lines.—During the two previous grades, the attention of the pupils has been directed, so far as the lessons relate to lines, to their *shapes* only, as straight, crooked, curved, waved, and spiral. Now it is desirable that they should be taught the *positions* of lines, as vertical, slanting, horizontal. When the attention of the children is first directed to the *position* of lines and of objects, the terms, "up-and-down," "upright," "standing," etc., may be used for the purpose of illustrating the term *vertical;* and the common terms "leaning," "slanting," to illustrate the term *oblique;* and "lying down," "level," "even," to illustrate the term *horizontal.* As soon as the pupils clearly understand the proper terms for these positions they may be required to use them. Care should be taken to lead the pupils to apply the names of these positions to *objects* as well as to *lines.*

Qualities.—It will be noticed that *qualities are to be illustrated,* that objects having the given quality in a prominent degree are to be shown, and the pupils led to observe the quality, and to discover the same quality in other objects. The spelling of the words representing the objects and the qualities illustrated, may be taught whenever they are adapted to the grade.

Color.—In lessons on color, the name should first be associated with the *color* which it represents, by showing the given color and requiring the pupils to point it out on the chart, and among colored objects. To recite names and descriptions of colors, without also knowing the color when seen, is of no use.

Animals.—During these lessons on animals, let the names of both the animals and their flesh be written on the blackboard as the children mention them, and the spelling of each be taught when appropriate.

Drawing and Writing.—Let the teacher of the class select each day six slates from those pupils who have made the most commendable improvement in drawing and writing, and place them on her desk for inspection by the principal. If properly managed, this plan will prove a good incentive to improvement in neatness in the drawing and writing.

THIRD GRADE.

OUTLINE COURSE.

READING.—The last half of a First Reader, or the first half of a Second Reader. The tone of voice to be natural. The pupils to tell, in their own language, what they have been reading about.

Punctuation.—The use of the hyphen, apostrophe, and quotation-marks.

Elementary Sounds.—The sounds in words of one syllable to be given, and silent letters mentioned.

Definitions.—The meaning of words to be given, chiefly by their use in phrases or short sentences.

Spelling.—Words from the reading lessons, and other familiar words; also, writing short words from dictation.

ARITHMETIC.—*Numeration* through nine places; also, writing numbers through 100,000,000. *Addition*, on slates, examples of two, three, four, and five lines through millions; also, two, three, and four columns of eight or ten figures each.

Mental Arithmetic.—Simple, practical questions in addition and subtraction.

Oral Drills for rapid combinations of numbers.

Roman Numbers.—Their combinations to 200.

Multiplication Table.—Through 6 times 12.

OBJECT LESSONS.—Review the previous grades, and add, in *Form*, parallel lines, perpendicular lines, acute angle, obtuse angle, right angle, triangles, prisms, pyramids, circumference, diameter, ellipse, plane and curved surfaces.

Objects and Qualities.—The principal parts, shape, color, uses, and materials of common objects to be distinguished. The qualities—elastic, flexible, liquid, solid, combustible, absorbent, etc., to be illustrated.

Comparative Size.—The terms large and small, long and short, thick and thin, wide and narrow, deep and shallow, tall and short.

Color.—The common names of the prominent colors, shades, and tints.

Human Body.—The principal bones.

Animals.—Their movements, their food; also, the common classes, as beasts, birds, fishes, reptiles, insects.

Plants.—Names of common trees, plants and flowers; also, of common fruits and grains. The principal parts of trees to be mentioned.

DRAWING AND WRITING.—Drawing plane figures, also, lines in given positions; lines to be divided into three equal parts.

Writing.—Simple words; the formation of capitals; also, how to write the pupil's name.

N. B.—The exercises of this grade, upon a single subject, should not exceed thirty minutes at one time.

DIRECTIONS, &c.

READING.—The exercises for teaching reading may be divided into *three steps :*

First, training the pupils to know the words at sight.

Second, attention to the thoughts expressed.

Third, reading in easy, conversational tones.

The pupils may be trained to know the words at sight by writing them in columns on the blackboard—by pronouncing them from their books, commencing with the last word of the paragraph and proceeding in an order the reverse of that pursued in reading.

As soon as the words are known readily at sight, *chief attention should be given to the thoughts expressed.* The pupils may be led to attend to the thoughts expressed by requiring them to find out what the sentences tell—what the reading is about. The teacher may aid them in this matter by asking questions similar to the following : What does that sentence tell us ? What do the words in the next sentence say ? Who can tell what the next paragraph is about ?

When the pupils have accomplished the first two steps in a given reading lesson, they will be prepared to take the *third step,* and will readily learn to read with easy, conversational tones.

Punctuation.—The uses of the hyphen, apostrophe, and quotation-marks should first be explained from the blackboard, then examples of their use should be pointed out by the pupils in their reading books.

Elementary Sounds.—When the pupils can distinguish and make the sounds in words of one syllable, they may be required to tell which letters have no sound in given words ; also, to name the vowel sound by its number ; as in the word *make, m-a-k,* make, *a* has its first sound, the *e* is silent.

Definitions.—See remarks for the fourth grade.

Spelling.—Care should be taken in oral spelling to have each pupil pronounce the word before spelling it, to name each letter distinctly, to make a pause between the syllables, and to pronounce the word again when all the letters have been named.

In selecting familiar words it would be well to request the pupils to name words for the teacher to write on the blackboard, and all the class, afterward to copy these on their slates. But teachers should not depend entirely upon the words given by the pupils; they should add to the list other appropriate common words.

ARITHMETIC.—In this grade, the pupils should be so trained in *Numeration* that they can name any place at sight, in order and out of order; also, give the order of any place when its name is mentioned.

Notation.—In notation, the pupils should be taught to write readily and plainly, from dictation, any number through hundreds of millions.

Addition.—On commencing addition, in the Third Grade, the pupils should be taught "to carry;" at first, by means of short examples; afterward let the examples be made longer gradually, more difficult ones being given by extending both the length of the lines and of the columns. Give many more examples with a few long columns than with long lines. Care should be taken not to embarrass children by giving them *long and large* examples in addition before they can readily add short ones. Let the training be thorough in each step, and the progress gradual. The work of each succeeding week ought to embrace larger examples than were given during the previous one, and to furnish sufficient practice to enable the pupils to master all the difficulties.

Special care should be taken to train children in habits of *adding without counting.* One of the most effectual means toward securing this habit is to teach the pupils to give special attention to the figure that will represent the *units* as each successive number is added. The suggestions given in the Fourth Grade, relative to this point, will indicate methods that may be successfully used in the Third Grade. The names given to the answer in addition should be taught in this grade.

Mental Arithmetic.—The language used by the pupils should be sufficient to render the solution and answer to the question clearly intelligible to a listener, yet so brief as not to retard, unnecessarily, the process of mental calculation. Appropriate forms for answering questions in Mental Arithmetic, in the Third Grade, may be seen in the following examples :

If a coat cost $15, and a hat $5, how much will both cost? *Ans.* Both will cost the sum of $15 and $5, which is $20.

Henry had 8 marbles and bought 4 more, how many marbles had he then? *Ans.* Henry then had the sum of 8 marbles and 4 marbles, which is 12 marbles.

A boy had 9 apples and gave away 5 of them; how many apples had he left? *Ans.* He had 4 apples left; because, when 5 apples are taken from 9 apples, 4 apples will remain.

Oral Drills may be continued as in the Fourth Grade, and the pupils taught all the combinations by the addition of two numbers below 100, that will give each of the following figures, viz.: 0, 1, 2, 3, 4, 5, 6, 7, 8, 9.

The class may also be trained to add several numbers, and each pupil to write the result on a slate, or give it orally. The teacher may say 7+3+4+5+6+4+2+4+5, are how many? Each pupil, having added these numbers mentally, should write the sum obtained on the slate, and the teacher should then ascertain which pupils have performed the addition correctly.

Multiplication Table.—In teaching the Multiplication Table, it is very desirable that each step be thoroughly mastered before taking the succeeding one. This table may be first illustrated by means of balls on the numeral frame, by arranging the balls in groups of *twos* then of *threes.* When the groups of *twos* have been illustrated by the balls, the teacher may write the table of twos on the blackboard, thus:

First Form.	*Second Form.*
2 times 2 are 4	3×2= 6
3 " 2 " 6	6×2=12
4 " 2 " 8	9×2=18
5 " 2 " 10	4×2= 8
6 " 2 " 12	7×2=14
7 " 2 " 14, etc.	5×2=10, etc.

Let the pupils copy and learn the *First Form,* so as to repeat it, both forward and backward. Afterward place the *Second Form* on the blackboard, and let the pupils give each answer orally; also copy the table and write the answers. When the table of *twos* has been learned in both forms, teach the table of *threes* in the *First Form,* then in the *Second Form,* and afterward *review* both of them, in combination, in a *Third Form,* somewhat as follows:

2×2=	8×3=	3×3=
6×3=	5×2=	9×3=
4×2=	7×3=	8×2=
5×3=	6×2=	3×2=
9×2=	4×3=	2×6=
2×3=	7×2=	3×4=

All the tables may be taught on the same plan—first in order, then out of order, then by combination with the tables previously learned. New tables should not be presented before the pupils have learned thoroughly each preceding one through the *three forms.*

Roman Numbers.—In this Grade, the Key to Roman Numbers should be explained to the pupils, and numerous applications of it made to a variety of combinations, viz.: When letters representing equal values stand side by side, and when a letter representing a smaller number stands on the *right*-hand side of one representing a larger number, the values of each are to be added, as II *two,* XX *twenty,* VI *six,* XV *fifteen,* LX *sixty,* XXX *thirty.* When the letter representing a smaller number stands on the *left*-hand side of one representing a larger number, the value of the *left*-hand letter is to be taken from the value of the *right*-hand letter, as the value of I is to be taken from the value of V in the combination IV, which gives *four,* the number represented by IV; the value of X taken from the value of L in XL gives *forty* as the number represented by XL, etc. Training the pupils in numerous applications of this key will save much of the time usually spent in memorizing the Roman Numbers.

OBJECT LESSONS.—*Form.*—In teaching pupils what constitutes parallel lines, lead them to notice the fact that they are *side-by-side;* that they are the *same distance apart at all points;* afterward, in a subsequent grade, they can easily be led to observe that both lines extend in the same direction; also, that they can never meet.

In previous grades, the pupils have become familiar with the terms sharp, square, and blunt, as applied to corners; use this knowledge to illustrate the different kinds of angles, and give the terms *acute, right, obtuse* to be applied to angles, instead of sharp, square and blunt. In explaining the terms relative to lines, angles, diameters, etc., each of them should be illustrated on the blackboard, and the pupils also required to represent them on their slates.

Lead the pupils to observe that all *prisms* have oblong sides, and all *pyramids* triangular sides; that prisms differ in the number of their sides, and in the shape of their ends; that pyramids differ in the number of their sides, and in the shape of their bases.

Objects and Qualities.—Pupils should be led to point out and name the parts of common objects, to tell the shape of the parts, and the uses, color, etc., of the objects. This exercise should be so conducted as to lead the children to form habits of describing readily the things which they see.

See remarks in Fourth Grade relative to *Qualities.*

Size.—This may be illustrated by various objects, as strings of different sizes and lengths, slips of paper of different lengths and widths, and small pieces of wood.

Color.—The lessons on color should be illustrated by colored cards, pieces of ribbon, silk, worsteds, or other objects.

Human Body.—It is important that the pupils should learn to point out the location of all the bones and the other parts of the body, for which they are taught names.

Animals.—The lessons on animals should at first be conversational, and of such a character as to lead the children to notice, when away from school, the various kinds of movements of different animals, as, walking, running, jumping, hopping, flying, swimming, etc.; so that they may be able to tell what animals move in a given manner.

After the teacher has led the children to observe the different classes of animals, as beasts, birds, fishes, etc.; by showing them pictures of each, let them be requested to give the names of some animals of each class which they have seen. The names thus given might be written on the blackboard in groups corresponding to their several classes.

Plants.—After talking with the children about different kinds of flowers, plants, grains, fruits, trees, etc., which they have seen, and after they are able to name several of those most common, their attention may be directed to different parts of trees, as, roots, trunk, branches, limbs, leaves, etc.

Drawing and Writing.—All necessary explanations and illustrations on this subject should be made by the teacher from the blackboard; afterward, attention may be directed more to the work of individuals of the class.

See suggestions on this subject for the Fourth Grade.

Teachers in all the Grades are hereby particularly cautioned against the practice of "Sing-Song Recitations," and of allowing the pupils to use *screaming tones* of voice during class exercises.

SECOND GRADE.

OUTLINE COURSE.

READING—In a Second Reader. Special attention to be given to the use of conversational tones in reading. The pupils should be required to tell, in their own language, the subject matter of the lesson.

Punctuation.—The common use of the principal marks; also, the use of *Italic* letters.

Elementary Sounds.—Sounds of words in common use to be given, with exercises for correcting indistinct enunciation.

Definitions.—The meaning of words in the lesson to be given, chiefly by their use in phrases and short sentences.

Spelling.—Oral and written.—Words from the reading lessons; also, other common words.

ARITHMETIC.—*Addition* and *Subtraction*, with practical examples. *Multiplication*, with multipliers from one to twelve, inclusive.

Mental Arithmetic.—Addition, subtraction, and multiplication, with practical questions. *Oral Drills* for rapid combinations of numbers.

Roman Numbers.—Completed.

Multiplication Table.—Through 12 times 12.

Common Tables.—United States Money, Time, Liquid and Dry Measures, and Common Weight (Avoirdupois) taught by illustrations, and, as far as possible, by the use of objects.

OBJECT LESSONS.—Review and continue the topics of the Third Grade, and add, in *Form*—pentagon, hexagon, heptagon, octagon, nonagon, decagon, arc, radius; forms to be described; also, common objects, by their shape.

Objects and Qualities.—The shape, size, color, uses, materials, and qualities of objects, and where obtained. The qualities soluble, fusible, congealed, fibrous, pungent, astringent, odorous, fragrant, etc., etc., to be illustrated.

Size.—Measures from one inch to one yard, with exercises in judging of these lengths.

Color.—Exercises for leading the pupils to notice colors that harmonize or look well together.

Human Body.—Names and uses of parts of the organs of sense; also, the uses of the bones.

Animals.—Where found; their uses, habits, structure, and common classes.

Plants.—Their parts and uses; kinds used for food; fruits, grains, and nuts used for food.

Occupations.—Trades, tools, productions, commodities, etc.

Place and Direction.—The pupils to be led to notice and describe the relative position of objects in the school-room.

DRAWING AND WRITING.—Simple lessons in drawing from copies or objects.

Slate-Writing.—Words and short sentences to be written from dictation; capitals to be used.

Pen-Writing.—The small letters in the order of their simplicity; also, simple words. Each child to be taught to write its name, with its age and the date.

DIRECTIONS.

READING.—Should the teacher find her class using monotonous or unnatural tones, several selections should be made of reading lessons that are composed chiefly of conversations. These may be used for training the pupils to read in easy, speaking tones. Afterward other selections may follow, and special care be taken to teach the pupils to read in a pleasant, colloquial style. Two extremes, as to the amount of reading which the class is taken over, should be avoided—that of keeping the pupils too long on the same lesson, and that of reading over many lessons without sufficient attention to the *matter* and *manner* of reading. The first extreme destroys the pupils' interest in this exercise, and prevents them from acquiring the habit of reading to gain information; the second leads to carelessness in manner, and the habit of reading without sufficient attention to the thoughts expressed.

[See remarks in the Third Grade for other suggestions on this subject.]

Punctuation.—The use of *Italics* should be illustrated from the blackboard first, and afterward attention directed to them in the reading lessons, while the pupils are required to tell why the Italic words are used.

Elementary Sounds.—Care should be taken, in conducting the exercises in sounds, to train the pupils in habits of distinctness of enunciation, and in the use of smooth tones of voice—uttering the separated sounds of words will aid in accomplishing the first, and making the sounds with varying pitches and different volumes of voice will aid in producing the second. Silent letters should be pointed out by the pupils.

Definitions.—Avoid modes of teaching that will allow pupils to give mere memorized definitions, without the ability to illustrate the meaning of the given words by their use in complete sentences. During the exercises in definitions, faults of language should be corrected.

Spelling.—See suggestions for spelling, in the Third Grade.

ARITHMETIC.—In this grade *Addition* should be extended to examples with from three to five columns of ten or twelve figures each, with occasional examples embracing millions, for practice in notation. Exercises for training the pupils to add without counting should be continued through this grade. These may be given from the blackboard, and also on the pupils' slates.

Subtraction, in this grade, may be taught in *three steps.*

First.—With short examples in which each figure in the subtrahend is smaller than the one above it in the minuend.

Second.—With examples in which it is necessary "to borrow" from the column of a higher denomination.

Third.—With examples having naughts in the minuend, making it necessary "to borrow."

The second and third steps may be illustrated by bundles

of sticks, or cents, dimes, and dollars; also on the blackboard by cancelling the figure borrowed from, and writing the remainder above it. But no form of illustration should be continued longer than may be necessary to enable the pupils to understand the process of subtraction.

As a second step, in borrowing, a dot may be placed over the figure in the minuend to indicate that *it* must be considered *one less* in the subtraction, as

4̇26̇3
1445
——
2818

The names used, as *minuend, subtrahend, remainder* or *difference,* should be taught in connection with the examples for practice in this grade.

Multiplication.—It will be well to divide the instruction in multiplication for the second grade into three steps:

First.—Give examples in which no single product will exceed *nine,* as

243	3,142	3,231
2	2	3
486	6,284	9,693

Second.—The examples may embrace numbers in which it is necessary "to carry" to the next column, with multipliers from 2 to 5 inclusive.

Third.—The examples may extend to millions, including some naughts in the multiplicand, with 6, 7, 8, 9, 10, 11, and 12 for multipliers.

The names of the *terms* used in multiplication should be taught in this grade.

Mental Arithmetic.—The forms of the answers, in this grade, may very properly employ more language than in the preceding grade. *Examples:*—A man paid $12 for a barrel of flour, $8 for a ton of coal, and $5 for a load of wood; how much did he pay for all? *Ans.* He paid for all the sum of $12, $8, and $5, which is $25.

A farmer paid $40 for a cow, and sold her for $36; how much did he lose? *Ans.* He lost the difference between $36 and $40, which is $4.

What will 5 oranges cost, at 4 cents each? *Ans.* If one orange cost 4 cents, 5 oranges will cost 5 times 4 cents, or 20 cents.

Oral Drills.—These may be continued in this grade by the methods mentioned in the directions for the third grade; also with subtraction combined in the examples.

Multiplication Tables.—These may be continued in the same form as in the third grade. When all the tables, from two to twelve, have thus been learned, they may be reviewed from the blackboard in the following form, reading them thus, 5 times 6 are 30; 6 times 5 are 30, etc.:—

5×6 are 30	....	6×5 are 30	
9×5 "	....	5×9 "	
7×6 "	....	6×7 "	
4×9 "	....	9×4 "	
6×12 "	....	12×6 "	etc.

Subsequently the teacher may review the tables by asking—How many *fours* make twelve? How many *fives* make fifteen? How many *sevens* make twenty-one? How many *eights* make forty? How many *nines* make seventy-two? etc.

Common Tables.—The tables of weights and measures should be introduced first, by talking with the pupils about their experience in the use of them, and by familiar illustrations given by this means. Thus the table of United States money may be illustrated by cents, dimes, and dollars; that of liquid measure, by what the children know about buying milk, etc., by the pint and quart; that of dry measure, by purchases at the grocery, by quarts, small measures, pecks, etc.; that of common weight, by buying butter, sugar, etc.; that of time, by observing the hours marked on the clock, and by attention to the days, weeks, months, etc.

After talking with the pupils about the uses of a given table, write it on the blackboard, and let the pupils repeat it; then they may copy the items on slates, both in the order of the table and in a different order. Continue the repetition and copying until the table is thoroughly learned. Each of the tables may be presented and learned in a similar manner.

TABLES FOR CLASSES OF THE SECOND GRADE.

United States Money.

10 mills make 1 cent.
10 cents " 1 dime.
10 dimes " 1 dollar.
10 dollars " 1 eagle.

100 cents make one dollar.
50 " " one-half dollar.
25 " " one-quarter dollar.

Liquid Measure.

4 gills make 1 pint.
2 pints " 1 quart.
4 quarts " 1 gallon.
31½ galls. " 1 barrel.

Dry Measure.

2 pints make 1 quart.
2 quarts " 1 small measure.
8 quarts " 1 peck.
4 pecks " 1 bushel.

Time Measure.

60 seconds make 1 minute.
60 minutes " 1 hour.
24 hours " 1 day.
7 days " 1 week.
30 or 31 days " 1 month.
12 months " 1 year.
52 weeks " 1 year.
365 days " 1 year.
100 years " 1 century.

Days of the Week.

Sunday,
Monday,
Tuesday,
Wednesday,
Thursday,
Friday,
Saturday.

Seasons of the Year.

Spring,
Summer,
Autumn, or Fall,
Winter.

March, April, May, Are the Spring months.
June, July, August, Are the Summer months.
September, October, November, Are the Autumn, or Fall months.
December, January, February. Are the Winter months.

Common, or Avoirdupois Weight.

16 ounces make 1 pound.
8 " " 1 half pound.
4 " " 1 quarter of a pound.
100 pounds " 1 hundred weight.
20 hundred weight make 1 ton.
2,000 pounds make 1 ton.

In reviewing these tables, the teacher may question the pupils somewhat as follows: How many hours make a day? How many days make a year? How many days make a week? How many weeks make a year? How many minutes make an hour? How many months make a year? What is the shortest measure of time? What does it take to make the longest measure of time? How many quarts make a gallon? How many quarts in three gallons? How many quarts make a peck? How many pints in two quarts? How many quarts in two pecks? Which is more, one bushel or three pecks? How many ounces in half a pound of sugar?

A variety of similar questions may be asked after the tables have been learned in their order.

Roman Numbers.—Review and give further applications of the key, as indicated in the directions relative to this subject for the Third Grade.

OBJECT LESSONS.—It is not intended that each topic under this heading shall be made the subject of a lesson each day; but it is expected that a lesson will be given each day upon some one of these topics, and that these shall be varied so as to embrace all the topics of the grade during each month. Much more time and a greater number of lessons will be required for some of these topics than for others. This matter can easily be adjusted by the principal.

Form.—It is very desirable to have the manner of presenting the lessons on this subject varied in each succeeding grade, so as to avoid the possibility of memorizing and reciting any formula. To secure this end, let the reviews of the matter taught in preceding grades be so conducted as to compel attention to the shape of the various objects. As a means for accomplishing this, let the teacher describe the shape of a particular object, then request one pupil to point out that shape on the chart of forms, while another one selects it from the box of forms; then require the class to tell its name, and individual pupils to describe it, with the form before them.

By requiring the pupils to describe the shape of objects

placed before the class, the teacher will be enabled to test their knowledge of *form.*

Objects and Qualities.—Two distinct classes of exercises may be given under this heading. One consisting in training the pupils to distinguish given qualities, by using several objects having the same quality for illustration; the other, which is more appropriate for review exercises, requiring the pupils to ascertain what qualities a given object possesses. Instruction on this subject can not be considered complete without the use of both of these classes of exercises, in their proper order.

Size.—The pupils will obtain clear perceptions of size, and of length, by being required to judge of the size and length of objects before them, and of lines on the blackboard, then to measure these and ascertain the approximate correctness of their estimates. Drawing lines of given lengths on the slate, followed by a careful measurement of them, is a valuable means for training pupils in accuracy in determining size and length by the eye.

Color.—The lessons on color, for the second grade, should lead the pupils to perceive that some colors appear well when placed side by side, while others do not. For this purpose lead them to compare *red* and *green* with *blue* and *green; blue* and *orange* with *yellow* and *orange; yellow* and *purple* with *blue* and *purple,* or *red* and *purple.*

Human Body.—In teaching children the names and uses of the organs of sense, and their parts, special effort should be made to lead them to understand the subject by means of observations made with their own organs of sense. The actual seeing, hearing, feeling, tasting, and smelling of objects teach children facts which it is impossible to convey to their minds by means of the memorizing of language, however thorough and precise.

Animals.—The lessons on this subject should lead the children to notice the most distinguishing points in the structure of animals, and to see how their structure is adapted to their habits of life; for instance, how the webbed feet of some birds fit them for swimming, and how the long legs of others fit them for wading; how the strong claws and strong beaks of some birds enable them to feed on flesh; how the cushion-like feet of the cat enable it to walk noiselessly about in search of its prey; how the teeth of the cat and dog are fitted for tearing flesh, while those of the rat and squirrel are formed for cracking nuts and gnawing hard substances.

The chief aim of these lessons being to train the pupils in habits of observing nature, so that they may be enabled to gain therefrom the most useful knowledge, the exercises should be conducted in such a manner as to lead them to notice accurately the structure and habits of the various animals that come within their own observation. The facts thus learned should be, by the aid of the teacher, properly classified, as a foundation for subsequent study of the same subject.

Plants.—The lessons on plants, in this and the following grade, may appropriately lead the pupils to learn the most common *shapes of roots*, as turnip-shaped, branching, fibrous, conical, tuberous, etc.; also the *shapes of leaves*, as needle-shaped, arrow-shaped, egg-shaped, heart-shaped, hand-shaped, etc.; also the common *shapes of flowers*, as funnel-shaped, bell-shaped, pink-shaped, butterfly-shaped, helmet-shaped, cross-shaped, etc.; also the *parts and uses of leaves, flowers*, etc., as the stem, veins, blossom, petals, seed-vessels, etc.; also kinds of fruits which the pupils have seen—the names to be written on the blackboard, and copied by the pupils on their slates, as a spelling exercise. The names of fruits and grasses used for food, etc., may be written in groups. Like the lessons on animals, these exercises should be so conducted as to lead the pupils to form habits of carefully studying nature, as a means of pleasure and as a source of knowledge; therefore, the time selected for giving the lessons on plants, etc., should be during the seasons when the pupils can personally examine these objects.

Occupations.—The exercises on this topic should cause the children to ascertain the names of tools used in different occupations, and what is done with these tools; also what articles are made or produced. For instance, the teacher might write on the blackboard the word carpenter, shoemaker, or painter, and request the pupils to ascertain what tools are used by those who pursue the given trade, and report on the next day after the subject is thus assigned—the teacher writing the names of tools mentioned by the pupils on the blackboard, and the pupils copying them subsequently on their slates. These exercises will furnish an excellent opportunity for practice in observation, and, in describing what has been seen. They may be made useful, also, for first lessons in composition writing.

Place and Direction.—The exercises in this subject should be conducted with a view to prepare the pupils for understanding the elementary steps of Geography.

First Step.—Train the pupils to observe and describe the position of objects on the table in front of them, using the terms right, left, front, back.

Second Step.—Train the pupils to notice and describe the *positions* of the parts of the class-room, and of the principal articles in it, as: door, windows, blackboard, seats, table, chair, closet, etc.

Third Step.—Teach them the location of the streets near the school, and require them to observe and tell in what streets they go while on their way to and from school—the terms of direction, as east, west, north, south, may be introduced in this step. Represent these locations on the blackboard.

Drawing and Writing.—The lessons in drawing and writing, for this grade, must necessarily be simple, yet they should be progressive, and so arranged as to lead to a proper training of the eye and hand; indeed this training should be made a prominent object. The blackboard should be used much in illustrating the exercises of both drawing and writing. Enlarged copies of good drawing cards may be made on the blackboard, and the pupils required to copy them on their slates. Simple objects may be drawn on the blackboard by the teachers, then the same objects drawn by the pupils on their slates.

Care should be taken to teach the pupils proper positions for sitting, for holding their slates, also for the hand and fingers in holding the pen or pencil.

When writing is commenced with ink, do not confine the pupils too long to making the simple *elements* of letters; let them learn to write simple words as soon as practicable. It is not necessary that the pupils should write all the lines under each copy of the common writing-book. Whenever the pupils have made sufficient progress to be able to proceed with the next copy in order, let them go on with it—but there should be system in the progress; all the pupils in the grade should receive instruction relative to the same points, and write the same words simultaneously; thus all will attend to the same thing, at the same time, and proceed to a new lesson together.

Before leaving this grade, the pupils ought to be able to write simple words neatly with the pen; and to write their own names, and their age; also the day of the month, and the year, in a proper form for dating a letter. They should also be able to write familiar words, and short sentences from dictation, readily and plainly.

FIRST GRADE.

OUTLINE COURSE.

READING.—Lessons of the grade of the last half of a Second Reader. The expression to be natural. The pupils to state, in their own language, the subject matter of the lesson.

Punctuation.—Reviewed.

Elementary Sounds.—Words to be analyzed by sounds; the names of sounds given; faults of enunciation corrected.

Definitions.—The meaning of words to be given, chiefly by their use in phrases or short sentences, oral or written.

Spelling.—Words of the reading lessons; also familiar words and short sentences from dictation, orally and by writing on slates.

ARITHMETIC.—*Addition and Subtraction* reviewed; *Multiplication* extended to multipliers of four figures; *Division,* both long and short forms, with divisors from 2 to 25. Practical examples to be given in each of the rules.

Mental Arithmetic.—Division; also reviews in each of the rules, with practical examples. *Oral Drills* continued.

Roman Numbers.—Reviewed.

Division Table.—Taught in connection with a review of the multiplication table.

Common Tables.—Review those of the Second Grade, and add Long, Cloth and Surface measure; also a miscellaneous table.

OBJECT LESSONS.—Review and continue the topics of the Second Grade. The shapes of objects to be compared, and their resemblances and differences stated.

Descriptions of Objects.—Objects to be described by their shape, color, and obvious qualities.

Properties of Objects.—The properties which distinguish minerals, vegetables, and animals, to be illustrated.

Human Body.—Review the lessons of the previous grades, and add parts, and uses of the skin, food, etc.

Animals.—Their habits, and the adaptation of their structures to their habits; also a simple classification of common animals by their structure, as animals with hoofs, claws, webbed feet, etc.

Occupations.—Exercises to give the pupils habits of observing and describing common productions, commodities, etc.; also to give them ideas of the exchange, and sale of these.

GEOGRAPHY.—*First*, teach the points of the compass; then the location and direction of the most prominent objects near the school, and of the principal places in the city and its vicinity.

Second.—The definitions relating to the forms of land and water, from cards, blackboard and outline maps.

Third.—The name of the city, State and country in which the pupils live, and of the places in the vicinity of the city, with the location of the country shown on a globe and upon outline maps. Teach the shape of the earth, and the location of the principal countries of the world by means of a globe and hemisphere maps, and by associations with their most familiar animals, productions and inhabitants; also the location of the warm and the cold countries.

DRAWING AND WRITING.—Drawing continued as in the Second Grade.

Slate-writing.—Continued, with the use of capitals, period, hyphen, and question mark. Writing sentences from dictation.

Pen-writing.—Writing in books, from copies. The name of the pupil, and the date, to be written on the last line of each page as it is completed.

DIRECTIONS, ETC.

READING.—For suggestions relative to methods of teaching reading in classes of the First Grade, see remarks on this subject for the Second and Third Grades.

• *Elementary Sounds.*—The phonic analysis of words should train the pupils readily to distinguish and make all the sounds in given words, also to determine which letters are silent. It should also lead the pupils to such habits of distinctness in articulation as will remove the fault of neglecting to sound the final consonants, as *d* in an*d*, sen*d*, *r* in fa*r*, ca*r*, *ing* in sing*ing*, eat*ing*, etc.; also the errors of sounding improperly both consonants and vowels in the pronunciation of common words.

No other means is so efficient for training the organs of speech in clearness and correctness of articulation as that of elementary sounds. By suitable exercises with these, the ear and the vocal organs may be successfully cultivated, and the means furnished to each pupil for determining what are the correct sounds of the language, how to produce them, and the ability to cultivate their own organs of speech and tones of voice.

Care needs to be taken, in each grade, to prevent the pupils from making the short sounds of *a*, *e*, *i*, *o* and *u*, too long, when sounded alone. Let each of these sounds be made *very* short, as heard in, *at*, *net*, *it*, *not*, *nut*.

As a method for training pupils to distinguish the *silent* letters, let them first *sound* a word, giving each sound as heard when the word is properly pronounced,—then *spell* it, naming each letter in order,—next tell which letters have no sound. The pupils should also be required to tell what sound each letter has in given words, and to make the sound.

Definitions.—Exercises in which the definitions are to be written on slates, in short sentences, should be introduced in alternation with oral exercises of a similar character. It is desirable that an oral exercise of this kind, given as a lesson, on one day, should be followed on the next day with the same words to be defined in a written exercise, thus training the pupils to write as well as to talk.

In the oral definitions, let the pupils be required to tell what given words mean, in their own language, as well as to use them in short sentences. One pupil may be requested to give a brief definition of a word, another pupil to use it in a sentence, and another one to illustrate its meaning by describing its use. Habits of reciting formal, memorized definitions would be avoided by using thus several modes of giving the meaning of the same word, and the pupils would learn to define, and use words intelligently.

Spelling.—More attention should be given to written than to oral spelling, in this grade. Words may be dictated for the pupils to write on their slates; short sentences may be given for the same purpose; the pupils may be requested to write the names of classes of objects, as names of kinds of food, articles of clothing, of furniture, kinds of tools, names of occupations, of animals, of trees, of fruits, of articles that may be purchased at a grocery, etc., etc. These exercises will enable pupils to learn the spelling of a large class of words in common use.

ARITHMETIC.—*Addition* and *Subtraction*. It is intended that the *processes* of adding and subtracting shall have been taught so thoroughly, before the pupils are placed in the First Grade, that each one will be able to add and subtract with facility, and with a good degree of accuracy. Now, special pains should be taken to teach the *uses* of Addition and Subtraction by means of practical examples. A review of these rules should be had at least once each week, during the entire term of the First Grade.

Multiplication.—The first step, in this grade, may introduce each number from 12 to 20 as multipliers.

The second step may contain examples having larger numbers with two figures in the multiplier.

The third step may include multipliers with three or more figures; also multipliers containing naughts.

Pupils should be carefully trained *where* to write the first figure of each partial product. Both the multiplicand and multiplier should be so varied as to include all the difficulties arising from the different positions of naughts.

Division.—This may be most thoroughly taught by commencing with the "Long Division" form, and using a small number for a divisor. The following steps will indicate appropriate methods for teaching division.

First Step.—Give examples in which each figure of the dividend will contain the divisor without a remainder, as

```
2)486(243
  4
  —
  08
   8
   —
   06
    6
    —
```

Second Step.—Give examples, with the divisors less than *ten*, in which remainders will occur in the division, as:

```
8)9720(1215
  8
  —
  17
  16
  —
   12
    8
   —
    40
    40
    —
```

Third Step.—Extend the divisors to 15; also teach the "Short Division" form to be used subsequently in all examples where the divisor does not exceed 12. This step may include examples in which the quotient will contain a naught.

Fourth Step.—Give examples with divisors embracing numbers from 12 to 25. Arrange these examples so that the different quotients shall contain naughts in various positions.

Teachers should aim first to cause their pupils to understand the *processes* of the several rules, then to *use* them in an intelligent manner. The object of the drills, by means of numerous examples, should be *accuracy*, first; *rapidity*, second; never rapidity by neglecting accuracy. Practical examples should be given, in each of the rules, to insure a proper understanding of their uses.

Mental Arithmetic.—The forms for answering questions in addition, subtraction, and multiplication, in this grade, may be the same as for the Second Grade, which see. Questions may also be introduced which will require both addition and subtraction for their solution, as: Henry had 18 cents; he gave 2 cents for pencils, and 6 cents for a sponge; how many cents had he left? *Answer.*—Henry spent the sum of 2 cents and 6 cents, which is 8 cents. He then had left the difference between 8 cents and 18 cents, which is 10 cents.

Division.—How many tops at 3 cents each can be bought for 12 cents? *Ans.*—As many tops as 3 cents, the price of one top, is contained times in 12 cents, which is four times; therefore *four* tops can be bought.

If 2 apples cost 4 cents, what will one apple cost? *Ans.*—If 2 apples cost 4 cents, one apple will cost one-half of 4 cents, which is *two* cents.

Oral Drills.—These may embrace combinations with multiplication, addition, division and subtraction, as: $6\times5+6\div4+9-4+6$ are how many? See also suggestions for oral drills in the previous grades.

Multiplication and Division Tables.—These may be so combined that the Division Table will be readily learned from the Multiplication Table, thus:

4 × 7 are 28.	4 in 28 seven times,
7 × 4 " 28.	7 in 28 four "
6 × 7 " 42.	6 in 42 seven "
7 × 6 " 42.	7 in 42 six " etc.

The teacher may ask: How many *eights* in 32? How many *sevens* in 56? etc.

Tables of Weights and Measures.—These may be taught, as in the Second Grade, first, objectively, then memorized. All the tables of both the Second and First Grades should be reviewed thoroughly, in their order, and out of order.

TABLES FOR CLASSES OF THE FIRST GRADE.

LONG MEASURE.

12 inches	make	1 foot.
3 feet	"	1 yard.
16½ feet	"	1 rod.
5½ yards	"	1 rod.
40 rods	"	1 furlong.
8 furlongs	"	1 mile.
320 rods	"	1 mile.
3 miles	"	1 league.

CLOTH MEASURE.

3 feet make	"	1	yard.
36 inches	"	1	"
18 "	"	½	"
9 "	"	¼	"
4½ "	"	⅛	"
4 quarters	"	1	"

SURFACE MEASURE.

144	square	inches	make	1 square	foot.
9	"	feet	"	1 "	yard.
30¼	"	yards	"	1 "	rod.
160	"	rods	"	1 acre.	
640 acres			"	1 square mile.	

MISCELLANEOUS TABLE.

12 things	make	1 dozen.
144 "	"	1 gross.
12 dozen	"	1 "
12 gross	"	1 great gross.
20 things	"	1 score.
24 sheets	"	1 quire of paper.
20 quires	"	1 ream.
32 pounds	make	1 bushel of oats.
48 pounds	make	1 bushel of barley, or buckwheat.
58 "	"	1 " " corn.
60 "	"	1 " " wheat.
196 "	"	1 barrel of flour.
200 "	"	1 " " pork, beef, or fish.
280 "	"	1 " " salt.

After these tables have been thoroughly learned in order, the teacher may conduct brief reviews of the tables of both the First and Second Grades, by questions somewhat like the following:

How many inches in three-quarters of a yard? How many yards in one rod? How many rods in a mile? How many square inches in a square foot? How many buttons in a gross? How many sheets of paper in a quire? How many in half of a quire? How many pounds in a barrel of flour? Which is heavier, a bushel of wheat or a bushel of corn? How many pounds in half of a ton? How many pecks in two bushels? How many quarts in two gallons? How many days in a year? How many months in half of a year? How many square feet in a square yard? Which is longer, six feet or two yards?

OBJECT LESSONS.—Means are furnished for thoroughly developing the minds of children by the various topics embraced in Object Lessons, which are far more effective than any exercises that pertain exclusively to reading, spelling, arithmetic, etc. Children whose powers of mind have been developed by object lessons, so that they observe, compare, classify, and describe intelligently whatever comes within the range of their observation, will learn every subject more easily than they could have done without such training. For these reasons the teachers of the classes in each grade are directed to give suitable attention to all the topics embraced under the head of Object Lessons; also to keep prominently in view the importance of these lessons as a means for proper mental discipline, and not to regard the knowledge gained by the exercises as their chief value.

Due attention to these considerations will lead teachers to regard, as of much importance, the *manner of giving* the lesson.

Form.—The character of the instruction in this subject, especially so far as it pertains to learning to recognize and describe the various *forms* and *solids*, need not differ materially in the First and Second Grades. However, when the several shapes required have been learned, by means of the regular *forms* and *solids* provided for this purpose, the time given to this topic should be chiefly devoted to comparing and describing other objects by their shape, stating wherein those compared resemble each other, and wherein they differ.—See suggestions relative to *Form* for the Second and Third Grades.

Description of Objects.—This includes descriptions as indicated in the remarks under the head of *Form*, and also requires that the *color* and most obvious *qualities* of the objects described be mentioned, in addition. In this connection, it is desirable that the pupils be led to consider what qualities are necessary in the substances used for various tools, utensils, articles of dress, etc. For instance, what quality is necessary for wagon and other springs? What qualities make sponge useful? What qualities render salt and sugar valuable? What qualities give value to India rubber? What qualities give value to glass? What to steel? to iron? Why will not lead make good springs or knives?

Properties of Objects.—The lessons under this topic should cause the pupils to consider wherein animals, vegetables and minerals differ from each other. As a *first step* toward accomplishing this, require the pupils to observe slate-pencils, pieces of stone, iron, lead, chalk, and various pieces of wood, small plants, etc., and then tell what can be done with the wood and plants, that can not be done with stone, iron, etc. Also lead them to consider whether both of these classes of substances are obtained from the same source, and whether the iron and stone grow as the wood and small plants do. When the most obvious differences between these two classes of substances have been perceived by the pupils, give the term *Mineral* as the name for one class, and *Vegetable* as the name for the other.

Second Step.—The teacher may next call attention to the three great classes of substances—mineral, vegetable, and animal—and lead the pupils to observe and to tell what animals and vegetables can do (as take food, breathe, grow, die), which minerals cannot do.

Third Step.—Let the pupils be led to notice what animals generally can do which vegetables generally can not do (as move from place to place by their own power), also to observe the differences between the food of plants and that of animals; as that plants feed on minerals, or simple substances from the earth and air, while animals feed on vegetables and other animals.

The pupils might also be taught that substances which once formed a part of an animal, as wool, hair, bone, skin, are called *animal substances;* that wood, bark, gum, sugar, that once formed a part of a vegetable are called *vegetable substances.*

Human Body.—The lessons in this grade should be conducted so as to review the facts learned in previous grades, and also so as to extend the pupils' knowledge of the laws of health, especially so far as these pertain to the condition of the skin, habits of cleanliness, and the manner of eating.

Animals.—The manner of conducting the lessons on this topic for the First Grade classes, may be nearly the same as that for the Second Grade, but the pupils should be led to consider a greater number of animals than in the previous one, and to observe more carefully the peculiarities of structure, etc., with a view to extending the pupils' knowledge of classification.

To aid the pupils in making groups of animals, by simple classification, let the teacher write on the blackboard the following and similar names for groups:

Hoofed Animals.	*Gnawing Animals.*
Animals with sharp claws and sharp teeth.	*Hard-shelled Animals.*
	Wading Birds.
Swimming Birds.	*Birds of Prey.*

Then request the pupils to give the names of animals to be written under each heading.

See, also, suggestions for the Second Grade.

Occupations.—The exercises on this topic may resemble those required for the Second Grade, which see. And in addition to the points to which attention is given there, let the pupils be led to consider the necessity for buying and selling productions and articles of manufacture; also how these are taken from those who raise or make them to those who want to use them.

GEOGRAPHY.—The *Points of the Compass* should be taught thoroughly, as the *first step* of the *First Class of Topics* in this grade. The pupils should be able to name any direction, as the teacher points, and to point in any direction named.

In connection with and following the instruction relative to the points of compass, lead the pupil to learn the location, and the direction from the school of the streets near the school; also of the prominent buildings, parks, depots, ferries, and other public places within the range of the children's observation. The teacher should represent on the blackboard the situation of the schoolhouse, and the location and direction from it of the places mentioned, and allow the pupils to copy the same on their slates.

Second Step.—The attention of the pupils may be given next to the location, and direction from the city, of the principal places, as cities, villages, islands, rivers, etc., in the vicinity of the city. Care should now be taken to call out the knowledge of individual pupils in relation to these places. Drawings should be made on the blackboard, as before, showing the relative location and direction of each place mentioned by the pupils; and the pupils allowed to make similar drawings on their slates.

Second Class of Topics.—While attention is given to the location of places in the vicinity of the city, the terms *river*, *bay*, *island*, etc., will be used. Let the meaning of these terms now be taught, also other similar ones, relating to the forms of land and water. In doing this, present a picture of the object, as an island, river, strait, etc., from a chart or blackboard; then show how the same or a similar object is represented on a map. Follow this with a definition to be learned by the pupils. As the characteristics of each form of land or water—as that *an island is land entirely surrounded by water*—are learned, require the pupils to point out on a map several representatoins of islands, omitting the names of the particular islands in this stage. Proceed in a similar way to teach all the definitions.

During this stage the instruction has for its chief object, training children to recognize the various forms of land and water, by means of their characteristic features, and to describe each by suitable definitions; hence the attention of pupils need not be directed to the names and location of particular islands, isthmuses, straits, bays, etc., at this time.

Third Class of Topics.—Commence the instruction relative to the names and location of particular places with the city and its vicinity. No fixed limit to the extent of this exercise can be given, since the length to which it can be profitably carried will depend, in some degree, upon the personal knowledge of the members of the class with the places. The teacher should aim, however, so to use the knowledge of those pupils whose personal visitations have made them acquainted with the locations of the greatest number of places, as to extend the knowledge of the other pupils.

Such attention should be given to the location upon a map of the city, and the relative location and direction from it of the chief places in its vicinity, that the pupils will be able to point them out on an outline map. The name of the city, of the county, and of the State in which the pupils live, should be taught, and their locations shown on a map.

Second Step.—Teach the *shape of the earth* by means of a globe. Lead the pupils to compare a marble with an orange, and both the marble and orange with a globe, and thus to notice that each one resembles the other in *shape* only; also that each differs from the other in *size*. By this means prepare them for understanding that the globe represents the earth only in *shape*. Follow this with some simple illustrations as to the comparative size of the earth.

Third Step.—Talk with the pupils about people of different races and nations, and point out on the globe, also on outline maps, the location of the countries where each may be found: as Africa, the home of the colored men; China, the home of the Chinamen; Germany, the home of Germans, etc. Proceed in a similar manner with the most familiar animals, and the most common productions of different countries. Give the name of the country, and show its location on a globe, also on an outline map. Point out Greenland as the home of the white bear ; Africa as the home of the lion, zebra, ostrich and camel; Australia as the home of the kangaroo ; Spain as the country where cork and raisins are produced ; South America as the country from which brazil-nuts and cocoa-nuts are obtained; West Indies as the place from whence we obtain oranges and bananas, etc.

By means similar to that herein described the pupils may be made to realize that *Geography* teaches them about the homes of the different people, animals, and productions which they have seen, and of which they have heard.

In addition to the foregoing, the names and locations of some of the principal cities of this country may be given, and their locations shown, as, Boston, Albany, Buffalo, Chicago, St. Louis, San Francisco, New Orleans, Washington, Philadelphia, etc.: also the names of some of the States and countries, as Connecticut, New Jersey, Pennsylvania, Ohio, California, Canada, Mexico, Egypt, China, Italy, France, England, etc.

The grand divisions, and the names of the oceans, and a few of the largest mountain ranges and rivers, may be given, as Andes, Rocky, Amazon, Mississippi, Hudson, etc.

The aim of the teacher should be to give the pupils a good, general idea of the *shape of the Earth*, of the different portions of it as the *homes of races of men*, also as the places where particular fruits grow ; and of some parts as having continuous cold weather, and others continuous warm weather. This object must be accomplished chiefly by oral instruction. However, the work may be facilitated by placing in the hands of the pupils suitable text-books on Geography, to be examined by the children *after* the lesson has been given orally by the teacher ; but in no case should the pupils be required to study a lesson in the book before the subject of it has been presented orally by the teacher, as above indicated.

Each lesson may be gone over a second time by the teacher, after the pupils have studied the subject in their books. The order of the lessons, the topics presented, and the general character of the facts taught should conform to the directions given here, without regard to the order of presentation in the text-books used.

Drawing and Writing.—See suggestions for the Second Grade, and extend the work as presented in the outline course for the First Grade.

General Directions relative to Instruction in the several Grades of the Primary Course.

Reviews.—Such a review of previous lessons, in connection with each new lesson of the same subject, should be had as will cause the pupils properly to associate together the facts learned in all of them.

General reviews of subjects should be had at least once during each month. On these occasions the leading facts learned in previous grades, upon that subject, should be included.

Progress of Classes.—Whenever it is found that a class has advanced further in one or two subjects of its grade than it has in others, the principal of the school should direct the teacher to devote less time to the subject in which the class has thus advanced, and to give more time to the subjects in which the class has made the least progress. By this means the grade of the class may be equalized in all its studies.

No study of a succeeding grade should be introduced into a class of a lower grade, while that class has not completed the requirements of the grade in all its studies.

Progress of Pupils.—It often happens that two or three pupils do so far outstrip their fellows in a single month that it would be better, both for those pupils and for the class, to place these rapid learners in a class of the next grade above. Some such system might be adopted for making these transfers of the most advanced individual pupils, as the following: Announce to the class that at the end of each month, except the one preceding the examination for general promotions, two or three of the pupils who are found to have made the greatest progress will be promoted to the next class above. This would act as an incentive to progress upon all the members of the class; also aid in keeping the upper class full, while it would tend to relieve the generally crowded condition of the lower classes, where most of the pupils last admitted are placed.

Size of Class.—No class shall contain more than seventy-five pupils ; this is a very important restriction, and should be strictly observed by every principal.

Time Devoted to Recitations, Study, etc.—No class in the primary course should be required to spend more than half an hour, at one time, upon the same exercise.

The mind, as well as the body, needs rest. A change of subject, and a change in the manner of conducting class exercises, are both necessary to furnish opportunities for rest during school hours.

Taking Books Home.—No books shall be taken home, nor lessons given to be studied after school hours, in any class below the Second Grade.

Study at Home.—The two higher classes may be assigned a short lesson each day for study out of school ; but such lesson shall not be so long as to require a child of ordinary capacity more than half an hour to learn it. The chief object of these lessons should be to train children in habits of study and self-reliance.

Writing and Drawing.—Writing on slates shall be made a daily exercise. An exercise in writing with the pen shall be given twice a week, in the grades where it is prescribed. A lesson in drawing shall be given at least once each week, in all the classes.

Use of Pencils and Pens.—The pupils shall not be allowed to write with short pencils. Particular care must be taken as to methods of holding both pencil and pen, also as to the position of the body while writing.

Physical Training.—The pupils should be exercised, daily, in such a manner as to expand the lungs, develop the muscles, and impart an easy and graceful carriage to the body. Calisthenic exercises, to the utmost practicable extent, should be employed for the attainment of these objects.

Vocal Music.—Instruction in vocal music shall be given to the pupils in every grade.

Manners and Morals.—Such instruction should be given daily the children of all the grades as will foster a spirit of kind-ess and courtesy toward each other, a feeling of respect ward parent and teacher, and a love for cleanliness, order, w, and truth. The reading lessons and the ordinary incidents the school-room may be made the means of inculcating the eat moral truths common to all well-ordered minds.

Children learn to love and practice kindness, neatness, truth-lness, and politeness by observing these traits in those ound them. It is, therefore, exceedingly important that the acher should present living illustrations of these qualities, by er own conduct before the pupils, during all her intercourse ith the class.

Social relations, the dependence of each individual upon his ighbor—the necessity of labor—the benefits of society and vernment, should be illustrated and taught by means of easy d familiar lessons suited to the age and capacity of the ildren. As the development of the moral nature is of greater portance to the welfare of the individual and the community an any other part of education, no opportunity should be nitted for training children in such habits as will cause them grow up truthful, honest, self-governing, and law-abiding tizens.

COURSE OF INSTRUCTION

PRESCRIBED FOR

GRAMMAR SCHOOLS.

EIGHTH GRADE.

OUTLINE COURSE.

Reading.—Of the grade of a Third Reader (first half), with a review of punctuation, Roman numbers, and elementary sounds; and with exercises on the subject-matter of the lessons.

Spelling.—From the reading lessons, with miscellaneous words, and words derived therefrom; also exercises in writing words and short sentences from dictation. Particular attention to be given to the use of capitals.

Definitions.—From the reading lessons, to teach the meaning of the words, with illustrations by forming sentences; in no case to be committed to memory and mechanically recited.

Mental Arithmetic.—As far as in written arithmetic, to include exercises in the analysis of operations and examples, and in rapid calculation without analysis.

Written Arithmetic.—Through the simple rules and Federal money, with practical examples.

Tables of weights, measures, etc., reviewed, with practical illustrations and simple applications.

Geography.—Primary geography, including the general outlines, with definitions and illustrations, by means of the globe, of the form, magnitude, and motions of the earth, zones, etc.

Elementary Science.—By oral instruction, in the qualities and uses of familiar objects, such as articles of clothing, food, materials for building, &c.; also a knowledge of geometrical forms, with illustrations on the blackboard and by models.

DIRECTIONS AND SUGGESTIONS.

Reading.

1. The number of reading lessons carefully taught should bear a reasonable relation to the time the pupils have been in the grade. No selection, other than the best English poetry, should be so long dwelt upon and so frequently repeated as to render the exercise a mere recitation.

2. Should a large number of consecutive lessons in the Reader be of the same general character, a part should be omitted, so as to give variety of style and subject.

3. Where two or more classes are in different parts of the same grade, and use the same Reader, care should be taken to have a corresponding difference in their reading lessons.

4. Distinctness of articulation and the avoidance of all improper clipping of terminations, and of the omission or slurring of syllables, should receive careful and constant attention.

5. As a test of the general condition of the reading, classes should occasionally be called upon to read unfamiliar pieces of the same general grade.

6. New and difficult words should be carefully pronounced, and, if necessary, explained, before the piece or paragraph is read by the pupils.

7. Where a simple system of diacritical marks is used in the Reading Book, the pupils should be taught to understand and apply them.

8. Lists of common words liable to be mispronounced, such as *length* and *strength*, should be made by the teacher, and the class exercised upon them. The elementary sounds and their more difficult combinations of words and phrases, requiring great mobility of the vocal organs, especially *final consonants,*

should receive frequent attention. A daily exercise of *five minutes* would probably be sufficient in most cases. Particular attention should be given to pupils of foreign birth or parentage, so as to insure their mastery of the principal difficulties of English pronunciation. Phonetic drills are very useful for this purpose.

9. In the employment of concert exercises in reading, especial care should be taken to prevent any injury to the voice by harsh or unnatural tones.

10. When the character of the paragraph or of the lesson will permit it, the pupils should be accustomed to state, in their own language, the important facts, principles, and moral lessons therein taught. Words, phrases, or allusions should be briefly explained whenever necessary for the proper understanding of the piece read.

11. The voice and manner of the pupil should accord with the character and sentiment of the selection. All drawling, sing-song tones should be prevented. This is easily done when the pupils are led to understand and enter into the spirit of the piece.

12. An occasional brief review of the Roman numbers, and of the names and signification of the marks used in punctuation, should be required.

13. Where the *primary* object of the exercise is to teach elocution, it is advisable, quite often, to require all the pupils, except the one reading, to close their books, the teacher also, only using the book for occasional reference. In this way, both the teacher and the class will be better able to criticise, and the criticism will be more just and valuable. Besides, the pupils will all be kept on the alert to listen, and the one reading will unavoidably endeavor to pronounce correctly, enunciate distinctly, and emphasize naturally. Additional effect will be given to the exercise by requiring the pupils to reproduce, in their own language, the substance of what is read to them.

14. The successful application of these suggestions involves the necessity of carefully grading the exercises and selections, so that the pupils be not required to read pieces which are above their comprehension. This is a point of the greatest importance.

SPELLING.

1. The exercises should be both oral and written, but principally written.

2. The selections of words from the reading lessons should be so made that the class will not be prevented from advancing from one reading lesson to another with proper rapidity.

3. For purposes of review, teachers should keep lists of those words of the lessons in which a large number of mistakes are made by the pupils.

4. In oral spelling, care should be taken to name each letter distinctly, except in the case of the "doubles," which are to be distinctly pronounced as such, and not as "*d'blee*" for "*double-e*," "*d'blow*" for "*double-o*," etc.

5. "Miscellaneous words" will include the ordinary proper names of persons (not the surnames), words naturally suggested by those of the reading lessons, and common words of the daily life of the household, the shop, and the street.

6. "Therefrom" refers not only to the miscellaneous words but to those of the lessons also. The derivatives required are those and those only which are in the commonest conversational use. They may be readily obtained by calling upon the class to suggest them. The modifications of the primitives required in order to form them, should be taught.

7. The written exercises should be as neat as possible, care being taken to train pupils to habits of orderly arrangement of their work on the slate or on paper.

8. When sentences are given, particular attention should be paid to the ordinary troublesome monosyllables, to the proper use of capitals, the sign of the possessive case, the period, the interrogation mark, and the use of the hyphen in a word divided at the end of a line.

DEFINITIONS.

1. In selecting words for definition, two leading purposes should be specially kept in view: 1. To impress or illustrate the particular meaning of the word as used in the lesson; 2. To enlarge and correct the pupil's own vocabulary.

2. Very simple words, such as *father*, *water*, *knife*, *knee*, *book*, *child*, &c., the *meaning* of which every child must understand, should not, in the lower grades at least, be assigned for definition. Properly to define such words requires a nice discrimination in the use of language, and a minuteness of analysis beyond the powers of a young child. Teachers are apt to go astray in this direction. It is principally on this account that the limitation, "to teach the meaning of the words," has been introduced in prescribing this part of the grade. The written exercises will necessarily contain many such words, and thus the child will learn to spell them.

3. Where a word has, in common use, two or more meanings quite diverse, a separate oral illustration should be required for each; and where several words differently spelled have the same or a similar pronunciation, a separate construction should be required for each in the written exercises.

4. Defining one part of speech by another is a common error. It may be corrected or avoided by giving small groups of words, each consisting of a primitive and some of its most commonly used derivatives, and requiring, as an oral exercise, a phrase or a sentence to illustrate the use of each word in the group.

5. Teachers should be particularly careful to comply with

the direction, "in no case to be committed to memory and mechanically recited." The mere committing of dictionary definitions to memory, or the substitution for the word to be defined of another word, perhaps more difficult and unusual, is a perversion of the exercise. It is not only useless but pernicious, for it neither aids in mental development nor adds to the pupil's information, nor does it benefit him in his use of language.

6. At this stage of the pupil's advancement, a full exercise on a given word should comprise the following: 1. Pronounce it; 2. Use it in the construction of a phrase or a sentence; 3. Define it; 4. Write a sentence containing it. [For the whole class].

7. In the performance of the written exercises required for *definitions* in this grade, the pupils may not only be taught the meaning of the words, but, by a skillful application on the part of the teacher, be prepared for the exercises in *composition* subsequently prescribed. This point should be kept in view. Correctness in the use of words, propriety in the thought, the accurate use of capitals, punctuation marks, &c., should be invariably insisted upon.

Mental Arithmetic.

1. The mental arithmetic should both precede and accompany the written arithmetic, step by step. The principal distinction between these two divisions of the subject is, that when the numbers involved are too great or too many to be readily retained in the memory, the slate should be employed as an assistant.

2. "Exercises in rapid calculation without analysis" should, as far as possible, be of the most practical character. Examples given should be silently wrought by the whole class simultaneously as in written arithmetic, and the results obtained be written upon the slates, promptly, and at a given signal. The analysis can then be separately required of as many pupils as may seem expedient.

3. The explanatory or analytic statements made by the pupil should be of the simplest and most direct character consistent with clearness, and all unnecessary repetitions of formulæ be carefully avoided. Where this is not done, the principal effort of the pupil is to recall in due order the set form of words rather than to form the arithmetical combinations necessary to the solution.

4. Besides simple examples in the four fundamental rules and Federal money, very simple operations involving practical applications of the selected tables of money, weight, and measure, should constitute a portion of the exercises in mental arithmetic.

5. In the explanation or analysis of examples in mental as well as written arithmetic, the pupils should generally be called upon, before solving, to state the question.

6. Mental exercises in arithmetic should be conducted in a spirited manner. They should always have the character of extemporized exercises, and are in no case to form a part of the home-work of the pupil. (See By-laws, § 79.)

Written Arithmetic.

1. The slates should be kept in the best condition as to cleanness; the figures should be distinctly and neatly made, and written in lines parallel to the upper edge of the slate. A reasonable allowance should be made for imperfections in the forms of figures in those exercises where haste is required; yet, every effort should be made to fix in the pupils habits of care, neatness, and system in all that pertains to the written exercises.

2. Exercises in adding columns of figures should be given with such frequency as may be found necessary to produce and retain accuracy and rapidity.

3. Every form of counting, whether by fingers, dots, marks, or other devices, should be strictly prohibited, and the class should be frequently tested for this special purpose.

4. The pupil should be allowed to name only the successive results arising from the addition of the several successive figures, avoiding all that oral or mental repetition of the tables

which is known as the "spelling process," and all other unnecessary formulæ.

5. The above remark, in regard to the oral or mental repetition of the tables, applies to all the fundamental rules and their applications. The processes should be reduced to the most concise form practicable.

6. When pupils show an ability to add in two or more figures at a time, they should be encouraged to do so in exercises that are wrought out silently.

7. When the divisor is less than 13, the long division process is not to be employed or allowed.

8. Short practical examples, involving two or more of the rules, should frequently be geven, and in such a way as to cultivate the intelligence of the pupil.

9. Examples requiring a very large number of figures for their solution should be avoided except as far as they may be necessary in order to give practical expertness.

10. Examples should be given to test the pupils' accuracy in writing numbers requiring 0's, and their knowledge of the proper methods where the multiplier or divisor contains 0's.

11. Exercises should be given to insure facility in reading and writing Federal money, and in reducing, by *inspection* and *without analysis*, dollars, or dollars and cents, to cents or to mills, &c., &c., and conversely.

12, Analogous exercises in Federal money should be substituted for those in the simple rules referred to in the preceding sections, as soon as may be found expedient.

13. In all practical examples, instead of *telling* pupils to add, subtract, multiply, or divide, give the question in such a manner as to oblige them to exercise their own judment as to the method and principle to be employed.

14. No detailed analysis is necessary in addition or subtraction.

15. Give examples of bills of purchase or sale involving several items, and similar to those required in daily life.

16. Exercises in arithmetic are not to be assiwned for *home study*. (See § 79 of the By-laws.)

FORMS OF ARITHMETICAL ANALYSIS.

A. (*Fundamental*)—***Multiplication.***

Question.—If one yard cost $3, what will 4 yards cost?
Analysis.—If one yard cost $3, 4 yards will cost 4 times $3, which are $12.
Note.—Avoid the too concise form "will cost 4 times 3, which are 12."

B. (*Derived*)—*Division.* (1.)

Question.—If one yard cost $3, how many yards may be bought for $12?
Analysis.—If one yard cost $3, $12 will buy as many yards as $3 are contained times in $12, which are 4 yards.

Note.—Avoid the too concise form "as many as 3 are contained in 12."

C. (*Derived*)—*Division.* (2.)

Question.—If 4 yards cost $12, what will one yard cost?
Analysis.—If 4 yards cost $12, 1 yard will cost ¼ of $12, which is $3.

Note.—Avoid the very faulty forms "as much as 4 is contained in $12," or "times in $12," or "4 is contained in 12."

COMBINATIONS OF A, B, & C.

C and A. Division and Multiplication.

Question.—If 4 yards cost $12, what will 9 yards cost?
Analysis.—First by C for price of 1 yard, then by A for price of 9 yards.

C and B. Division. (2) *and* (1).

Question.—If 4 yards cost $12, how many yards may be bought for $27?
Analysis.—First by C for price of 1 yard, then by B for number of yards.

Note 1.—*Avoid set forms of giving questions.*—Vary the order of statement as far as is consistent with perfect clearness. For instance, the last question might have been put thus: Spent $27 for cloth. How many yards did I buy, if $12 bought 3 yards; or, how many yards for $27, if 4 yards cost $3? &c., &c.

Note 2.—It is frequently an assistance to some pupils to have them divide each question in *conditions* and *demand*—as in C and A. "The condition is, that 4 yards cost $12. The demand is, what is the price of 9 yards?" Such devices should be sparingly used.

TABLES OF MONEY, WEIGHT, &c.

The teaching of the *Tables of Money, Weight, Measure, &c.*, should be restricted to the following:

1. Federal Money.—The usual table, its notation, and halves, quarters, and eighths of the dollar. The difference between the full table and money of accounts. Adversely to the use of the terms *shilling* and *penny.*

2. *Length*—12 in. = 1 ft., 3 ft. = 1 yd., 5½ yds., = 1 rod, 220 yds. = 1 furlong, 8 furlongs, or 1,760 yds., or 5,280 ft. = 1 mile.

3. *Surface.*—144 sq. in. = 1 sq. ft., 9 sq. ft. = 1 sq. yd., 30¼ sq. yds. = 1 sq. rod.

4. *Solidity.*—1,728 cu. in. = 1 cu. ft., 27 cu. ft. = cu. yd., 128 cu. ft. = 1 cord of wood.

5. *Dry Capacity.*—2 pts. = 1 qt., 8 qts. = 1 peck, 4 pecks, or 2,150 cu. in = 1 bu., 36 bus. = 1 chaldron.

6. *Liquid Capacity.*—4 gills = 1 pt., 2 pts. = 1 qt., 4 qts., or 231 cu. in. = 1 gall.

7. *Avoirdupois Weight.*—7,000 grs. or 16 oz. = 1 lb., 100 lbs. = 1 cwt., 2,000 lbs. or 20 cwt. = 1 ton, 2,240 lbs. = long ton, or old ton.

8. *Troy Weight.*—24 grs. = 1 dwt., 20 dwt. = 1 oz., 12 oz., or 5,760 grs. = 1 lb.

Time-table and Calendar.—Explain leap year. Tell time by the clock.

10. *Miscellaneous Table.*—Teach *dozen, gross, score, quire, ream.*

GEOGRAPHY.

General Suggestions.

1. It is of the first importance that geography should be so taught and reviewed, as not to leave in the mind of the pupil a mere collection of facts, without mutual relation or dependence. On the contrary, the pupil should, from the first, be taught to consider the *earth* as man's dwelling-place—its *motions* as bringing him the necessary vicissitudes of day and night, and the changes of the seasons—its *land-surface* as the chief theatre of animal and vegetable life—the *ocean* as the world's broad

highway, and the exhaustless source of clouds and rains, so necessary to every form of life on the land-surface—the great permanent *air-currents*, as carrying to the land this moisture from the sea—the *mountains* as its condensers, as well as the chief source of mineral wealth—the *springs* and *rivers*, with their branches, as carrying back again, and over the land, the ever circulating water of the ocean—and of *cities* and *towns*, not as black dots on a map, in colored patches, which he has learned to call countries, perhaps near some crooked black streaks, which he has learned to call rivers, but as the centres of social life and development, the seats of government, and the crowded, busy hives of human industry and intelligence.

When geography is thus taught, it is one of the most interesting, important, and practical of studies; but, if it is taught chiefly as a description, by unvarying formulæ, of long lists of rivers, capes, peninsulas, boundaries, &c., supplemented, perhaps, by a precise, verbatim repetition of the descriptive geography, as contained in even the very best text-book, it is one of the dullest and most unprofitable.

2. The text-book is a most important, and even indispensable *auxiliary*, but there is no more common and pernicious error, than that of *substituting it in place of the teacher*, who thus is degraded into a mere stupid, profitless, and mechanical *hearer of lessons*.

Primary Geography.

"*Primary Geography and General Outlines*" should include only such topics as may readily be taught by means of a blackboard, a small and simple globe, and an outline map of the hemispheres. It is of great importance that the pupil's first impressions be formed from the globe, rather than from the flat and distorted representation of the map.

Part 1*st*. (The greater part of this is a review of the geography of the highest primary grade. It is to be *tested* in review, by placing the pointer in the hand of the pupil.)

The *form of the earth*, its *magnitude*, the *continents* and *grand divisions*, their relative positions, their connecting isthmuses, and a few of their most important projections—the *oceans*, their positions, and principal arms and islands—five or six of the great *mountain systems* of America, and from eight to ten in the rest of the world; three or four well-known *volcanoes* —about a dozen each of the chief *rivers* and *straits*, and about half as many great *lakes*—from ten to a dozen of the most important *cities* of the world, and in a very general way, the location of the most important countries, such as the *United States*, *Great Britain*, *Germany*, *Japan*, *China*, *&c.* With each of these cities and countries some interesting or important *fact* should be at once associated.

Part 2*d*. (To be taught as facts, in the simplest outline, and without attempting to explain according to any of the hypotheses of scientific physical geography, but by using the map and globe, whenever necessary, to impress any particular statement on the pupils' minds.) A *brief* notice of the *ocean currents*, their direction, temperature, and use, pointing out only the equatorial current, one Arctic current, one Antarctic current, and the Gulf stream—the *trade winds* (very briefly), their location, direction, use in commerce, and their influence (in assisting to produce the great South American rivers, the Nile, &c.)—a general notion of *climate*, as affected by distance from the equator, and by elevation—the *motions of the earth*, and the *inclination of its axis*—the *zones*, their limits, and a very few of their well known and characteristic plants and animals, and, in a very general way, the location of the *chief races* of mankind.

Only such definitions should be included as are strictly elementary, and found necessary in teaching the points assigned to the grade.

Elementary Science.

(By Oral Instruction.)

General Suggestions.—1. The *leading object* in this branch of instruction is to cultivate habits of *observation and reflection*, and to give *facility in oral description*. Avoid everything tending to convert these lessons into recitations of set forms of words, however these forms may have been obtained, however well they may be understood by the pupils, and however important the facts thus stated.

2. "*Familiar objects,*" and familiar animals, plants, and minerals take precedence of all others in the selection of topics.

It is neither possible nor desirable to attempt to teach all, or even the greater part of the topics that might be classified with the requirements of any grade. No topic should be treated exhaustively, nor should the topics selected be so few or so frequently reviewed as to narrow down or suspend the discipline of the observing faculty. The selection and limitation are left to the good sense of the teacher.

3. The *objective method* of teaching presents two distinct though intimately related departments. *Perceptive* teaching, in which the object, as an acorn or an egg, is directly presented to the pupils' senses; and *Conceptive teaching,* in which impressions previously received are recalled, arranged, and utilized, the objects themselves not being presented to the senses during the lesson. An oak, an elephant, or a thunder-storm, would fall under the latter department.

The use of pictures, models, or other sensible representations of objects, is an important combination and modification of the two principal methods, and should be often employed.

4. *Definitions* should be very sparingly introdnced, and *never* in the first stages of a subject. *If given at all* they should sum up knowledge already attained. The terms *organic, inorganic, vegetable, animal* and *mineral,* are prominent among the very few terms requiring definition. Such definitions should be prepared for by a process at once inductive and objective.

5. No fact which the teacher can *readily* lead the pupil to discover for himself should be imparted by the teacher. *Important* facts not readily derived from the pupil's own observation, must of course be supplied by the teacher. Avoid

overloading a topic by details. No topic should be selected in which the number of *facts to be told* bears a large proportion to those which the pupil may be *led to discover* for himself.

6. *The language used by the pupil must be entirely his own*, excepting, of course, the few indispensable definitions.

7. The *process employed* will present two distinct stages: *First, the* analytical or preparatory, in which the teacher leads the pupil by questions to discover or to remember the properties or peculiarities of an object, or to state any other important facts associated with it. The responses by the pupil will be, of course, in his own words; and the additional statements which the teacher himself may find necessary to make, will be given in the form of conversations. This stage gives the principal discipline of the powers of observation and reflection.

The points thus considered and the facts thus stated should be written upon the black-board in the briefest possible synoptical form, but each only *after* it has been considered. While some such synopsis is *indispensable* to the *teacher* as the first step of *preparation* for giving the lesson, it should never be presented to the *pupil* except by the *gradual* process above indicated.

8. The *second* or *review stage* of the process is based upon the results of the *first*, and furnishes the principal discipline of the powers of description or oral statement. The facts already considered should be re-arranged, if necessary, into an orderly synopsis upon the black-board, the pupils being called upon to assist in this arrangement. Pupils should then be required, in turn, to state what they can recall of each item of the synopsis, then of each group of items, and, lastly, of the whole subject. Then the synopsis may be wholly or in part removed or hidden, and the oral process of review repeated. *As a final stage*, and before dismissing the subject, an extempore *composition*, with or without the aid of the synopsis upon the board, should be written by each pupil upon his slate.

Eighth Grade.—The oral instruction in this grade necessarily bears a close relation to that of the highest primary grade, to which and to the above "General Suggestions" for Elementary Science, the teacher is referred. The *geometrical forms* should be drawn upon the slate by the pupils. Each class in this grade should have a box of geometrical models. The lessons on these forms should alternate with those upon "the qualities and uses of familiar objects."

SEVENTH GRADE.

OUTLINE COURSE.

READING.—Of the grade of a Third Reader (latter half), with exercises as in the Eighth Grade.

Spelling and Definitions.—From the reading lessons, with exercises in miscellaneous words and sentences, as in the previous grade.

Mental Arithmetic.—As far as in written arithmetic, with exercises in analysis and calculation.

Written Arithmetic.—A review of Federal money; common fractions commenced; simple operations to be taught, with practical applications, avoiding difficult or complex examples.

Tables of weights and measures reviewed and applied.

GEOGRAPHY.—Outlines of North America, including the United States and West Indies, with the descriptive geography of those countries; only conspicuous or important localities to be taught; elementary definitions and illustrations continued, with the addition of latitude and longitude.

ELEMENTARY SCIENCE.—By oral instruction; the qualities and uses of familiar objects; also an outline knowledge of zoology.

DIRECTIONS, &c.

READING, SPELLING, DEFINITIONS, AND USE OF WORDS, as in the *Eighth Grade.*

MENTAL ARITHMETIC, general directions, as in the Eighth Grade.

WRITTEN ARITHMETIC, as in the Eighth Grade—Directions 1 to 16. Also,

1. A *review of Federal money*, which forms a part of every grade up to the *fifth* inclusive, after which it blends with nearly all the other arithmetical exercises. It should form a part of the regular class work at least once a week, and at the monthly reviews. [See By-laws, § 80].

2. "Simple operations of common fractions" include such examples as are given below. "Practical operations" will include such simple applications as may be readily given in connection with the commonly used tables of money, weight and measure, &c.; as, "In $\frac{3}{8}$ lb. of sugar, how many oz."? "18 quarts are what part of a bushel?" &c., &c.

3. There is less difference between the mental and the written arithmetic in this grade than in any other. The same processes and forms of analysis should be employed in both.

4. In the written exercises, pupils should use the signs of operation, $+ - \times \div$, and the sign of equality, to indicate the work performed, and its result.

5. Omit "compound fractions" entirely. Such expressions as $\frac{1}{2}$ of $2\frac{2}{3}$, $\frac{3}{4}$ of $\frac{7}{8}$, &c., only involve the finding of a *fractional part*, and should be treated at first as such, rather than as a special kind of fractions. The same direction may be given in relation to "complex fractions," except in the case of such as have an *integral* denominator; as $\frac{2\frac{1}{3}}{5}$, read $2\frac{1}{3}$ fifths. &c. These can be readily reduced by multiplying both terms by the denominator found in the fractional numerator. All other cases of "complex fractions," so called, should be treated as *indicated division*. Such expressions as $\frac{7\frac{1}{4}}{9\frac{2}{3}}$ are not to be explained as fractions. A unit cannot be divided into $9\frac{2}{3}$ *equal* parts.

6. In this grade the subject of fractions should, as far as possible, be divested of technicalities, and be made to coincide with the acquired experience and simple notions of a child.

On this account, it is much better to say, *find* $\frac{2}{3}$ of $\frac{5}{8}$, than to say, *multiply* $\frac{5}{8}$ by $\frac{2}{3}$, or *find* $\frac{2}{3}$ *times* $\frac{5}{8}$.

SYLLABUS OF TOPICS FOR ARITHMETIC.

(With Suggestions and Examples.)

I.—The *idea* of a fraction developed *objectively.*

The *equality* of the parts to be very carefully illustrated.

The *relative value* of variovs fractional parts, *as greater or less.*

The *definition* of a fraction.

The *terms* of a fraction *defined* and the *order* of *statement.*

The *notation* of fractions and *location* of terms, or *order* of *writing.*

Exercises in writing and explaining fractions.

Fractional expressions *less* than a unit.

Proper fractions defined, and examples.

Fractional expressions *equal to* or *greater than* a unit.

Improper fractions defined and illustrated.

Exercises in writing proper and improper fractions.

II.—Fundamental Axiom $1 = \frac{n}{n}$

Reduction of units to improper fractions.—*Analysis* A. (Page 74.)

Reduction of mixed numbers to improper fractions.—*Analysis* A.

Definition of mixed numbers.

Exercises in mixed numbers, *limited to small denominators.*

Reduction of improper fractions to mixed numbers.—Analysis B. (Page 74.)

III.—Reduction of fractions *to greater denominatiors*—or higher terms. [What may halves, thirds, &c., be changed into? $\frac{1}{?}$'s? etc.] To be illustrated objectively.

Examples with greater denominators than can be solved by *inspection.*

Analysis C. (Begin with fundamental axiom.)

Term *Divisor* or *Factor,* with exercises in finding, by *inspection only,* a *Common Divisor* or *Common Factor.* Definition to be given.

Note.—Too great importance can hardly be given to this exercise of inspection. The application of the principle is indispensable in many of the arithmetical exercises in every succeeding grade. With proper training, it will become, within reasonable limits, a fixed mental habit, requiring no conscious effort.

Reduction of Fractions to Lower Terms, or *Less Denominators—Analysis C.* Exercises, &c.

Definition of "Lowest Terms"—Examples in finding what part one whole number is of another—corresponding examples in tables.

IV.—Multiple—term illustrated and defined.
Common Multiple " " "
Exercises, to be solved by inspection.

Reduction to Common Denominator—use two fractions only.
Application of common multiple to reducing to common denominator.
Distinction between common multiple and common denominator.
Definition of common denominator.
" " least common denominator.
Examples in reducing to least common denominators.

Analysis C.

Examples involving previous reduction to lowest terms.
Use of common denominator as the simple but indispensable basis for the working and explanation of Addition, Subtraction, and Division of Fractions.

V.—Impossibility of adding quantities with unlike names, illustrated: add 3 dogs and 4 cats; 3 animals+4 animals=7 animals.
Adding things of like names.
Adding fractions of the same denominator—Examples.

Adding fractions of different denominators—Examples—*Analysis C.*
Necessity of reducing to common denominator.
The numerators *only* added; why?

NOTE. In no example give more than two fractions. The common denominator to contain not more than two digits.

Addition of small mixed numbers—Examples—*Analysis C.*

NOTE. See that the *sign of operation* and the equality sign are not omitted. Avoid reducing to improper fractions.

Rule.—1st. See that the fractions are in their lowest terms; 2d. Reduce to common denominator; 3d. Add their numerators; &c.

Subtracting fractions of different denominators—*Analysis C.*

Rule.—1st. See that the fractions are in their lowest terms; 2d. Reduce to common denominator; 3d. Subtract their numerators; &c.
The same examples may be used as in addition.
Questions should be occasionally varied by asking, "Which is the greater," or "What is the difference?"

NOTE.—In mixed numbers avoid { 1st. Reducing to improper factions.
2d. The difficult case, $7\frac{1}{3}-2\frac{7}{8}$ [6th Grade].

VI.—"Multiplication of fractions" and "compound fractions" identical.
It must not be forgotten *by the teacher* that from the nature and definition of a fraction, every example in fractions must involve or relate to division in some way.
There are two cases in the so-called multiplication of fractions:

1st. Where a fraction or mixed number is to be actually multiplied. In this case the multiplier must be a *whole number*—as 3 *times* $\frac{2}{7}$, or 3 *times* 4 $\frac{2}{7}$.

2. Where a *fractional part* is to be taken of *either a whole number*, or of a *fraction*, or of both; as $\frac{2}{3}$ of 17, or $\frac{2}{3}$ of $\frac{5}{7}$ or $\frac{2}{3}$ of $7\frac{1}{2}$.

NOTE.—The so-called multiplication by a mixed number is a combination of the 1st and 2d cases.

Only in the first case should the expression "*times*" be used.

In the second case the expression "*of*" only should be used.

In the case of multiplying by a mixed number, the expression "*times*" is used for conciseness, though not logically correct. The proper expression is too cumbersome in practice—"*4 times the number, and ⅔ of the number.*"

Only the two varieties of the first case, and the first two varieties of the second case are required in the 7th Grade.

Examples:	
Multiplication OF Fractions.	7 times $\frac{3}{8}$——Analysis as in simple rule, then B. 7 times $4\frac{2}{3}$——Analysis as in simple ×, then B.
Multiplication BY Fractions =taking part=division:	$\frac{1}{8}$ of 24; $\frac{12}{36}$ of \$24 " " " $\frac{3}{8}$ of 25; $\frac{24}{36}$ of \$25 " " " $\frac{3}{8}$ of $\frac{5}{7}$; $\frac{12}{18}$ of $\frac{4}{6}$ " " D.

Examples to be given in the *practical form* at as early a stage as can be made expedient.

Find how many cents, or cents and mills, in a given fraction of a dollar.

Occasional examples involving preliminary reduction to lowest terms.

Rule.—1st. See that the fractions are in their lowest terms. 2d. Multiply the numerators for new numerator, and the denominators for a new denominator.

Solutions by direct *cancellation* are not required of this grade.

VII.—There are two cases in the *Division of Fractions:*

1st. Division of a fractional number, as, $\frac{3}{8}\div 7$, and $4\frac{3}{8}\div 7$; evidently identical with $\frac{1}{7}$ of $\frac{3}{8}$, and $\frac{1}{7}$ of $4\frac{3}{8}$ in the so-called multiplication of fractions.

2d. Division of any number, integral or fractional, by a fractional number, as $5\div\frac{7}{8}$, $\frac{5}{6}\div\frac{7}{8}$, $8\frac{5}{6}\div\frac{7}{8}$, $8\frac{5}{6}\div 9\frac{7}{8}$.

The form of putting the questions should be varied as much as possible, so as to train pupils to select and apply the right principle and method.

When the *divisor* is less than the *dividend*—"*How many times* is $4\frac{3}{8}$ contained in 7?

When the *dividend* is less than the *divisor*—"*What* is the one-seventh *part of* $\frac{3}{8}$?

Also, "*How much* is $\frac{1}{7}$ of $\frac{3}{8}$? And least frequently the technical form "*Divide* $\frac{3}{8}$ by 7," "*Divide* $\frac{5}{9}$ by $\frac{2}{7}$?

The two varieties of the 1st case, and the first two varieties of the second case, are required in the 7th Grade.

Examples in Division of and by Fractions—Analysis:

The method and analysis to be by *common divisor.*

Rule.—1st. See that the fractions are in their lowest terms; 2d. Reduce to a common denominator; 3d. Divide the numerator of the dividend by the numerator of the divisor.

Examples in finding what part one fractional number is of another.

The method by inverting the divisor is deferred to the 6th Grade.

When the method is taken, its analysis will be required to prevent the mechanical procedure of using a rule, the principle of which is not understood.

Practical Examples: 1st Group.
- If a yard cost $\$\frac{7}{9}$, how much can be bought for \$8 ?
- " " " $\$\frac{7}{9}$, " " " " " " $\$\frac{5}{6}$?

2d Group.
- If $\frac{3}{8}$ yard cost \$5, what will a yard cost ?
- " $\frac{3}{8}$ " " $\$\frac{5}{6}$, " " " "

Forms of Analysis for the Seventh Grade.

Analysis A.—Example.—Reduce $5\frac{1}{2}$ to halves, or to an improper fraction:—$1 = \frac{2}{2}$; $5 = 5$ times $\frac{2}{2} = \frac{10}{2}$; $\frac{10}{2} + \frac{1}{2} = \frac{11}{2}$.

Analysis B.—Example.—Reduce $\frac{15}{2}$ to units, or to a mixed number:—$1 = \frac{2}{2}$; hence, in $\frac{15}{2}$ there are as many units as $\frac{2}{2}$ are contained times in $\frac{15}{2}$, equal to $7\frac{1}{2}$.

Analysis C.—Example 1.—Reduce $\frac{2}{3}$ to *ninths*:—In a unit there are $\frac{9}{9}$· hence $\frac{1}{3} = \frac{3}{9}$, and $\frac{2}{3} = 2 \times \frac{3}{9} = \frac{6}{9}$.

Example 2.—Reduce $\frac{6}{9}$ to *thirds*, or to its lowest terms:—$1 = \frac{9}{9}$; $\frac{1}{3} = \frac{3}{9}$; hence there as many thirds in $\frac{6}{9}$ as $\frac{3}{9}$ are contained times in $\frac{6}{9}$, or *two*-thirds—$\frac{2}{3}$.

NOTE.—Avoid saying "a whole number," or "one whole number," when speaking of a *unit.*

Question.—If a yard cost $\$\frac{3}{8}$, how much can be bought for $\$\frac{7}{9}$?

Analysis D.—(See Analysis B, 8th Grade, to be combined with reduction to Common Denominator.)

If a yard cost $\$\frac{3}{8}$, $\$\frac{7}{9}$ will buy as many yards as $\$\frac{3}{8}$ are contained times in $\$\frac{7}{9}$, or reducing to Common Denominator, $\frac{3}{8} = \frac{27}{72}$, $\frac{7}{9} = \frac{56}{72}$, as many yards as $\frac{27}{72}$ are contained times in $\frac{56}{72}$, or $2\frac{2}{27}$ yards.

NOTE 1.—To "invert the divisor and proceed as in multiplication," is much more concise as a method, but it is not in any sense an *analysis*, but a condensed and valuable *rule*, which is to be both taught and analyzed in the 6th Grade. When this concise rule is taught before the analysis by reducing to a common denominator, the teacher will usually find three undesirable results : First, the pupils are as likely to invert the wrong fraction as the right one unless the question is always put in one particular way, and even then, until after much practice, thus showing that they are not guided by any principle ; Second, they cannot explain the process ; and third, it is then much more difficult to teach the analysis, because their minds are preoccupied by the brief rule, which naturally seems to them so much more desirable, as it costs little or no mental effort.

As the study of fractions is an important mental discipline, any course which practically excludes the fundamental principle of division by a fraction should be carefully avoided.

NOTE 2.—It will be perceived that the analysis of the division of one fraction by another by the process of reducing to a common denominator, is essentially identical with the analysis of reducing an improper fraction to a whole or mixed number.

Question.—If $\frac{4}{7}$ of a yard cost $\$\frac{3}{5}$, what will a yard cost ?

Analysis E.—(See Analysis C, in 8th Grade, with which the following is essentially identical.)

If $\frac{4}{7}$ of a yard cost $\$\frac{3}{5}$, $\frac{1}{7}$ of a yard will cost $\frac{1}{4}$ of $\$\frac{3}{5}$ (note that this division by the numerator is the vital step in the process), which is $\$\frac{3}{20}$, and a yard or $\frac{7}{7}$ will cost 7 times $\$\frac{3}{20}$, or $\frac{21}{20}$, equal to $1\frac{1}{20}$.

NOTE 1.—This is one of the most important analyses in the entire range of the arithmetic of the grammar-school grades. If neglected, or badly taught, it seriously deranges the work

of the teachers of more advanced grades, where it must be so frequently applied. If the teacher will present it immediately *after*, and then *in connection with*, a review of Analysis C, and dwell particularly upon the *step noted in parenthesis*, a great part of the difficulty in fixing the entire process will disappear.

NOTE 2.—It is of course understood that the examples given to the class will not be confined to yards and dollars. Even the order of these should be at times inverted; as, in the problem last treated, we might have—

If $3-5 purchase 4-7 of a yard, how much will a dollar buy?

TABLES OF MONEY, WEIGHTS, &c.

1. Review perfectly the tables of the 8th Grade.

2. Add the following to *Long Measure*. Teach the *use* of each term: 4 in. = 1 hand, 3 feet = 1 pace, 6 feet = 1 fathom, $1\frac{1}{6}$ miles = 1 *knot*.

3. *Surveyors' Long Measure.*—4 rods, or 66 feet, or 100 links = 1 chain, 80 chains = 1 mile.

4. *Surveyors' Square Measure.*— 16 sq. rods = 1 sq. chain, 10 sq. chains = 1 acre 640 acres = 1 sq. mile or *section*, 36 sq. miles = 1 township.
Explain the use of *section* and *township*.

5. *Miscellaneous Avoirdupois Weight.*—60 lbs. = 1 bush. wheat, 196 lbs. = 1 bbl. flour, 200 lbs. = 1 bbl. beef or pork, 100 lbs. = 1 quintal of fish, $62\frac{1}{2}$ lbs. or 1,000 oz. = 1 cu. foot of water.

6. *Apothecaries' Weight.*—Show that its lb., oz. and grain are identical with those of Troy weight; that the only difference consists in the subdivision of the ounce. Teach its table and use.

7. *English Money, etc.*—The usual table. Teach the value of a *pound sterling*—$4.87. Teach the value of a *franc*—18 cents 6 mills.
If any foreign dollar is taught, let it be the *rix-dollar* of Prussia and North Germany = 69 cents.

8. *Angular Measure.*—Teach the following terms: *Circle, circumference, quadrant, radius, diameter.* Teach the notation. Give examples in reading, as 16° 17′ 45″.
60″ = 1′, 60′ = 1°, 90° = 1 quadrant, 360° = 1 circle, 360° = circ. of Earth, $69\frac{1}{2}$ miles = 1 degree of latitude, circumference of a circle = $3\frac{1}{7}$ times the diameter.

GEOGRAPHY.

"Elementary definitions and illustrations continued," in the review or completion of the geography of the Eighth Grade, "with the addition of latitude and longitude."

"*Outlines of North America.*" *First:*—Treat the continent *as a whole*, pointing out its separate countries, most important capes, peninsulas, islands, and arms of the sea; its divisions into mountains, plateaux, and lowland plains, naming only a few of the most important of each.

Iceland, Greenland, Alaska, and all other *Arctic Geography* to be treated very briefly, and chiefly with reference to climate resources and people.—*Newfoundland*, the *Dominion of Canada*, its surface, its provinces and territories, their climate resources and people, and our trade with them, the form of government, the capital of the Dominion and those of the provinces, and the other most important towns; the commerçial and international importance of the St. Lawrence river and the Great Lakes, and the small importance of the other rivers, of which three or four will be enough.

United States.—A simple outline will embrace the following:

1. *Local Geography.*—The boundaries of the country as a whole, its dimensions in round numbers, the location of the great mountain systems, the western plateaux [a section of the country roughly drawn in chalk upon the blackboard will be found efficient], the high western plain, the low central plain, the eastern slope, and the California basin; about a dozen of the chief rivers, with the great branches; about five or six each of the great lakes, bays and capes; about twenty-five of the principal cities, and the names of the several States and Territories, individually and in groups.

All local geography to be taught with the assistance of the outline map and the pointer, and to be reviewed with and without the map.

2*d. Descriptive Geography* will include a very brief description of the highlands, lowlands, and drainage system already pointed out; the climate and its gradual modifications by latitude, elevation, and distance from the sea, and a general statement of the leading agricultural staples, in the order of their latitude—rice, sugar, cotton, tobacco, corn and wheat.

The capitals and a few other details of the States may also be taught.

Mexico.—Its surface, climate, resources, and people; their language, government, and social condition; about five or six of the principal cities.—*Central America* very briefly; the names of its States and their capitals, and their general similarity to Mexico.—*West Indies*, the principal groups, about ten or a dozen of the most important islands; the climate, resources and people; their colonial relations, and their commerce with the United States, if important.

Outline Knowledge of Zoology.

In relation to this part of the grade, the following suggestions are made:—

1. Zoology being a science of *classification*, it is indispensably requisite to teach the distinctions upon which the classification depends.

2. Only the *simplest outline* need be taught, with such facts and details as seem most naturally appropriate to illustrate the subject.

3. The process of classification being naturally *objective*, that is, animals being classified by their obvious peculiarities, the pupil should be led, by an exercise of the observing faculties, to discover the peculiarities himself.

4. Well known typical animals should be taken as the *objective basis* of the classification; such as *man, monkey, bat, cat, rat, horse, deer, cow, and whale;—eagle, parrot, canary, rooster, ostrich, snipe, and duck;—turtle, alligator, rattlesnake, and frog;—perch, cod, shark, &c.;—bee, butterfly, beetle, &c.;—spider and crab;—squid, snail, and oyster;—star-fish, jelly-fish, and corals.*

5. The simplest names should be used, where possible, in preference to the more scientific, or, at least, as preparatory thereto; thus, it is better to use the term *four-handed* than *quadrumana; gnawers* than *rodentia; scratchers* than *rasores; two-winged* than *diptera;* &c. A few scientific terms, such as *mollusc* and *bivalve,* are in such common use that they may be readily explained and applied.

6. *Associated facts not strictly scientific*—such as the uses of animals, anecdotes concerning them, their peculiarities and habits, which the pupils have themselves observed—will form an indispensable part of these exercises.

7. The pupils should be encouraged to acquire as many facts as possible by their own observation and reflection. For this purpose the collection of animals in the Central Park may be employed to subserve an important educational purpose, and the pupils of our schools should be incited to the study of their habits and peculiarities.

8. The exercises should be *conversational,* the reviews frequent; the instruction should also embrace exercises in classifying well-known animals from a miscellaneous list, giving the reasons in each case. Too much ground should not be attempted at first.

9. Some system of *diagrams,* roughly sketched in chalk, will be found of great service in assisting the pupils to remember the classification. The best and simplest is, probably, that used in the ordinary "genealogical tree." The diagram should be gradually developed as the lessons proceed, and not the whole of it given in the preliminary stages.

10. No teacher can give such classified "outline" without having first, by careful study, acquired it. This can be readily accomplished from any of the school manuals on the rudiments of Natural History.

11. It is not expected that the classification should extend to *species* and *variety,* sometimes not even to *genera.* It is de-

sirable that pupils should have some definite ideas as to the relations of the following terms used in zoology: *kingdom, branch or type, class, order, family, genus, species, variety, individual.* These can be best exhibited by a diagram, but should in no case be presented by formal definition. All but the last four should be mentioned in describing any given animal.

12. The exercises should include a portion, at least, of the topics suggested in the following synopsis, which is here presented for the guidance of the teacher. This synopsis comprehends three successive outlines, each complete in itself or with that preceding it:

First General Outline.—Distinction of organic and inorganic objects taught objectively. Difference between animals and plants. What is an *organ?* An animal? Four great *types* of animals (Cuvier's, omitting the *protozoa*). Exercises in classifying, by *types* only, such animals as the *dog, lobster, clam, coral, shad, wasp, goose, star-fish, garter-snake, shrimp, toad, tortoise, oyster, &c.* The reasons of the classification should be given in each case. Each type to be then briefly defined. Why vertebrates are placed first.

Second General Outline.—*Classes of Vertebrates.*—(Tenney's arrangement is preferable, as being brief and simple.) Illustrate, as by types, by mentioning animals belonging to the several classes, mammals (those which feed their young with milk), birds, reptiles, batrachians (frog kind). Fishes; brief description of each class to be given. Name common vertebrates to be classified, occasionally mentioning an animal not a vertebrate, in order to test the attention and accuracy of the pupils; for example, *alligator, robin, mouse, worm, herring, toad, lion, jelly-fish, rattle-snake, elephant, flea, hawk, turtle, &c. &c.*

Classes of articulates to be treated very briefly, but in the same manner as the vertebrates. Simplest division, as *insects, crustacea,* and *worms,* to be employed.

Classes of molluscs—treat also briefly, by referring only to their general characteristics. Teach the meaning of the terms *univalve* and *bivalve.* Specimens of shells will be useful for illustration; but it must be remembered that the structure of the animal itself is far more interesting and important than that of the shell which incloses it.

Classes of radiates, probably treated with sufficient fullness in connection with types. Review if necessary.

Here it would be well to teach the classification of animals as *herbivorous, carnivorous* and *omnivorous;* also the general relations of the *teeth* of animals to other peculiarities, such as *feet, forms, food, digestive apparatus,* and *habits;* also as far as may be possible, illustrations of the importance of their several functions in nature.

Third General Outline.—In this many orders should be omitted because not readily treated objectively. The following embraces all that *may* be taught. Of course the whole cannot be taught to any one class.

MAMMALS.

Order 1.—*Two-handed* (*Bimana*).—To be treated briefly. The five races of men, with their characteristic peculiarities. The geographical distribution of each to be also briefly referred to.

Order 2.—*Four-handed* (*Quadrumana*).—A few examples, according to the experience of the pupils. Refer to the geographical distribution.

Order 3.—*Hand-winged* (*Cheiroptera*).—Use a drawing, or dried specimen, if one can be procured. Any interesting facts about bats, and their nocturnal habits.

Order 4.—*Insect-eaters* (*Insectivora*).—Omit altogether, except to *name the mole* as such, and refer to its small, hidden eyes, etc.

Order 5.—*Flesh-eaters* (*Carnivora*).—To be treated more fully. Refer to general structure of teeth, feet, and stomach. Refer to *cat family*, using common cat as type; *dog family*, using dog as type; *weasel family*, their form, habits, etc., naming *sable, marten, ermine*, and *mink*, and referring to the value of their furs; *bear family*; also briefly to *seal family*.

Order 6.—(*Marsupials*).—Refer to the geographical distribution. The exception of the opossum.

Order 7.—*Gnawers* (*Rodents*).—Use the *rat* or *squirrel* as a type. Refer to peculiarity of teeth, and the provision for their continued growth. Teach about the *rat, mouse, squirrel, beaver, rabbit.* Refer to the *woodchuck, porcupine*, and *guinea-pig.*

Order 8.—*Thick-skinned* (*Pachyderms*).—Treat briefly of the *elephant*, the *rhinoceros*, and *swine* families; more fully of the *horse family*, including *horse, ass, mule*, and *zebra.* Geographical origin of the horse, its dispersion and influence in human affairs.

Order 9.—*Cud-chewers* (*Ruminants*).—Relations of food to teeth, stomach, feet, etc., etc. Teach three families: 1. *Deer family*, horns solid, deciduous; 2. *Hollow-horned family* (horns permanent); 3. *Camel family* (hornless.) Refer to *llama* and *vicuna.*

Order 10.—*Whale-like* (*Cetacea*).—Refer to fish-like character of whale; how dissimilar; its uses. The *porpoise* and *dolphin.*

BIRDS.

1. Birds of Prey (*Raptores*).—Vulture, falcon, owl, condor, hawk, eagle.
2. Climbers (*Scansores*).—Parrot, woodpecker, etc.
3. Perchers (*Insessores*).—Give a few well known birds as examples.
4. Scratchers (*Rasores*).—Gallinaceous birds and dove family.
5. Runners (*Cursores*).—Ostrich; its habits.

6. Waders (*Grallatores*).—Crane, stork, snipe, etc.

7. Swimmers (*Natatores*).—Duck family: Swan, petrel, penguin, albatross, etc. Refer to *nests* of birds, their *migrations, instinct,* etc.

Reptiles and Frog Family.—Treat very briefly, teaching something of turtles, crocodiles, and alligators, serpents and their fangs; the frog and its transformations.

Fishes.—Treat the classification very briefly; show distinction between the two groups, bony and cartilaginous fishes, with the orders spine-finned and soft-finned; also the shark and the sturgeon.

Articulates.—These present many advantages for the school-room. They are small, and easily procured for perceptive teaching. A simple microscope is a great assistant in awakening an interest. Of *insects,* collections of type specimens can easily be made. Only the simplest and most interesting facts, however, need be taught, The general characteristics of this class of animals should be explained—their structure and the functions of their chief organs. Their wonderful *transformations* should be explained and exemplified; difference between *insects proper, spiders,* and *many-footed articulates* (*myriapods*).

The following orders should be taught and exemplified:

1. *Membrane-winged* (*Hymenoptera*).—Including the *bee family,* the *ant family,* the *wasp family*; the *ichneumon family* their peculiarities, habits, and *instinct.*

2. *Scale-winged* (*Lepidoptera*).—Moths and butterflies, caterpillars, etc., clothes-moth, geometer.

3. *Two-winged* (*Diptera*).—Mosquito family, wheat-fly, house-fly, etc.

4. *Case-winged* (*Coleoptera*).—Beetle, fire-fly, weevil, etc.

5. *Half-winged* (*Hemiptera*); or bugs, cicadas or harvest-flies, tree-hopper, cochineal, boat-fly, etc.

6. *Straight-winged* (*Orthoptera*).—Cricket, katydid, locust, grasshopper.

7. *Net-winged* (*Neuroptera*).—Dragon-fly, May-fly. Refer to the white ants.

Spiders (*Arachnida*).

Many-footed insects (*Myriapods*).—Centipedes.

Crustacea.—Crab, lobster.

Worms.—Earth-worm.

Note.—It is important to distinguish carefully the three terms, *insect* (*i.e.,* six-footed [hexapod], or true insects), *arachnids,* or eight-footed spiders and scorpions, and *myriapods,* or many-footed millipeds and centipedes. In using a representative of one of these groups as an object, it should be the primary aim to establish the obvious characteristics by which they are distinguished, firmly in the pupils' minds. Thus, in the insect proper, the body is divided into three divisions—the head, the body (or thorax), and the hind-body (or abdomen). The head is furnished with feelers (*antennæ*); the body supports three pairs of legs, and generally one or two pair of wings; the abdomen shows more or less clearly a number (seven) of rings or joints. In the arachnids, the head and body are consolidated into one division, which has no antennæ, supports four pairs of legs, but no wings. In the myriapods, the entire body consists of a series of very similar joints, not grouped into divisions separated (insected) from one another, but of which the first serves as a head, whilst each of the others, however numerous, supports either one or two pair of more or less imperfect legs.

SIXTH GRADE.

Outline Course.

Reading.—Of the grade of a Third Reader, with the exercises of the preceding grade; particular attention to be given to clearness of articulation and naturalness of intonations and general style.

Spelling.—Oral and written as in preceding grades.

Definitions.—As in the preceding grades, with easy exercises on the prefixes and suffixes, and their applications.

Mental Arithmetic.—As far as in written arithmetic, with exercises as in the preceding grades; also practice in the application of the arithmetical tables.

Written Arithmetic.—Through common fractions with their simple applications; including also a review of Federal money, and practice in the simple rules to secure rapidity and accuracy.

Geography.—Of the United States in detail; localities as in the preceding grades, with a brief description of each State and Territory.

Elementary Science.—By oral instruction. The uses and qualities of familiar objects continued; also an outline knowledge of botany, including the general structure and common uses of plants.

DIRECTIONS, &c.

Reading.—As in previous grades.

Spelling.—As in previous grades, with the following additional suggestion:

The selected names of important cities, states, and countries, which occur in the geographical lessons of the class, and especially such as are in frequent use in post office addresses, should form a part of the *miscellaneous words* taught in this grade; also familiar personal names, generally.

Definitions.—As in the previous grades, with the following:

"The easy exercises on the prefixes and suffixes" should be with *English primitives* at first, without regard to the etymology of those primitives. The affixes of Anglo-Saxon origin will therefore be taught first; afterward the meaning of such as *ab, con, pre, pro, sub, ion, ent,* &c., may be taught as illustrative of the diversity of meaning of such words as *abstract, subtract, concede, accede, precede,* &c. Also as showing that, for example, all words having the prefix *sub* convey the signification of *under*, and all having the suffix *ion* mean the *act of.*

2. Each group, with its radical or primitive, after being written on the slate or black-board, should be made the subject of an oral exercise in definitions, in order to impress upon the pupils' minds the modifications of meaning produced by the affixes. Their exemplifications in sentences should be also carefully attended to.

Mental Arithmetic.—See General Directions in the Seventh and Eighth Grades.

Written Arithmetic.—1. Particular care should be taken in the selection of examples that no one of them be so intricate and prolix as to consume a large amount of time, without affording any exercise of thought by the application of arithmetical principles.

2. Too much importance, nevertheless, can scarcely be given to the requirement of "practice for *rapidity* and *accuracy* in Federal money, as well as the Simple Rules of Arithmetic. To this should invariably be assigned a brief portion, at least, of the time given to every lesson in this subject. No part of the arithmetical discipline has a higher utilitarian value, whether for the purposes of practical life or for progress in the more advanced portions of the study; for nothing is more discouraging to the pupil than to find that, in any exercise involving other than a few figures, his results are almost always incorrect, from a want of habitual accuracy in performing the simple combinations involved in the elementary rules. Teachers are, therefore, especially advised to employ every variety of proper stimulus to make the exercises for this purpose thorough and effective.

3. In order to explain what is to be the special work of this grade, the following *syllabus* is here given. It will be observed by this, that this grade is much in advance of the Seventh, which it comprehends, chiefly in the form of mental exercises.

SYLLABUS OF TOPICS.

Systematic *Review of Definitions* of terms used in fractions, *with illustrative examples.* Omit complex fractions having fractions in the denominator.

Examples in finding the Greatest Common Factor of numbers by inspection.

Examples where the factor *cannot* be readily found by inspection, as 292 and 365 --315 and 572.

The result always should be tested or proved in accordance with the definition or Common Factor or Common Divisor.

Reduction of Fractions to their Lowest Terms.

Examples to be reduced by inspection ; $\frac{1200}{1800}$, $\frac{250}{750}$, *Analysis.*

Examples involving the special method of finding the Greatest Common Factor ; as $\frac{292}{365}$, $\frac{315}{572}$, &c., &c. Not too long.—*Analysis.*

Reduction of Improper Fractions and Mixed Numbers.

1st. Examples solved mentally or by inspection.

2d. Examples with larger numbers.—*Analysis.*

Examples in finding what part of one number is of another; as $7\frac{1}{3}$ is what part $9\frac{1}{2}$? \$$4\frac{3}{4}$, what part of \$$7\frac{2}{3}$? $\frac{17}{50}$ what part of $\frac{28}{29}$?

Examples in finding the Least Common Multiple of Two or more Numbers—and Definition.

1st. By inspection, as 5, 3, 2 ; 10, 20, 30.

2d. When not readily solved by inspection, as 28 and 39 ; 72, 25, 88 ; 6, 12, 18, 24, 36, and 48.

Statement of method or rule.

Relation of Least Common Multiple to Least Common Denominator.

Distinguish carefully between the two, and define each.

Examples in reducing to Least Common Denominators.—*Analysis.*

Give occasional examples involving preliminary reduction to lowest terms by inspection.

Examples in Addition of Fractions and Mixed Numbers.—Analysis.

Say " *Reduce to Least Common Denominator,*" rather than " *Find the Least Common Multiple of the Denominators.* Of course the latter forms a *part of the process* of the former.

Examples in Subtraction ; as $\frac{7}{15}$—$\frac{5}{17}$, $87\frac{1}{5}$—$29\frac{10}{26}$.

Make both kinds of examples as practical as possible.

Practical Examples (not too long), each involving both addition and subtraction.

NOTE.—Teachers should remember, that Arithmetic is not only a *science*, but also a practical *art ;* that this art involves important *devices*, many, or most, of which have been already taught, and their principles explained. These devices, such as reducing to lowest terms, cancellation, rejecting terminal 0's of a divisor, should not be at any time lost sight of. Examples in the special subject of the grade should be occasionally given of such a character as to require these devices. The omission or neglect of these important matters will be a serious defect in the character of the instruction given.

Principle of *Cancellation.*

Its *identity* with dividing by *common factors,* and with *reducing to lowest terms.* Show this by examples in fractions.

Examples of simple applications of cancellation to whole numbers.

Multiplication of Fractions..

Give examples where cancellation cannot be applied.—*Analysis.*

$\frac{12}{19}\times\frac{7}{25}$, $3\times\frac{43}{97}$, $\frac{17}{25}+144$, $16\frac{3}{8}\times12\frac{4}{7}$, abstract and *practical.*

Give examples that should be done by cancellation.—*Anaylsis.*

$125+\frac{4}{15}$, $\frac{24}{36}$ of \$17.38—39 barrels cost \$84, what will 26 barrels cost?

If a ton of hay cost \$$17\frac{1}{5}$, what will $\frac{25}{43}$ ton cost?

If 1 acre cost \$$23\frac{4}{7}$, what will $19\frac{1}{11}$ acres cost?

(*a.*) In this grade pupils should be made familiar with the following principle and its applications. It is frequently the most convenient method of solution.

$\frac{3}{8}$ of a number are equal to $\frac{1}{8}$ of 3 times the number, &c., &c.

$\frac{3}{8}$ of $40=\frac{1}{8}$ of 3 times 40.

Division of Fractions.

1st. Review and apply the method by *common denominators.*

2d. Review thoroughly its analysis.

3d. Teach carefully the following analysis, giving a variety of short examples to fix it thoroughly.

4th. Teach the brief and useful device of *inverting the divisor*, but in no case let the analysis of the rule be forgotten. Let it be given by the pupils as often as may be found necessary to insure its retention. The teacher is again reminded of the importance of the proper application of the principle of repetition of mental effort.

Example—Divide $\frac{3}{8}$ by $\frac{5}{7}$.

Begin with a unit for the dividend and apply the principle of *common divisor.* $(1\div\frac{5}{7})=)\frac{7}{7}\div\frac{5}{7})=\frac{7}{5}$, which quotient, it will be observed, is the *divisor inverted.*

Therefore $\frac{3}{8}$ of a unit$\div\frac{5}{7}=\frac{3}{8}$ of $\frac{7}{5}=\frac{21}{40}$.

Give examples where cancellation cannot be applied:

$\frac{17}{33}\div\frac{25}{49}$; $13\frac{1}{3}\div1\frac{2}{7}$. { At \$$1\frac{2}{7}$ a yard, how many yards can be bought for \$$13\frac{1}{3}$?
If $5\frac{2}{3}$ bushels cost \$$18\frac{4}{7}$, what will 1 bu. cost?

Give examples where cancellation is to be applied:

$23\frac{1}{3}\div12\frac{8}{11}$; $21\frac{3}{7}\div2\frac{19}{28}$, &c.

Give short examples involving simple combinations of the multiplication and division of fractions; also addition or subtraction, with multiplication or division, like the following:

Bought $7\frac{2}{3}$ yards and $3\frac{4}{5}$ yards at \$$1\frac{2}{3}$ a yard; cost of the whole?

Bought 36 yards, kept $9\frac{4}{5}$ yards, sold the remainder at $\$\frac{2}{9}$ a yard; how much did I get for it?

If I had sold it for $\$7\frac{1}{3}$, how much a yard would that be?

If $\frac{2}{3}$ yard cost $\$\frac{5}{7}$, what will $\frac{8}{11}$ yards cost?

If $\frac{2}{3}$ yard cost $\$\frac{5}{7}$, how much can be bought for $\$5\frac{2}{9}$?

Forms of Analysis.

Question.—If $\frac{4}{7}$ of a yard cost $\$\frac{3}{5}$, how much can be bought for $\$\frac{7}{8}$?

Analysis.—Combination of E and D. (Page 74.)

Question.—If $\frac{4}{7}$ of a yard cost $\$\frac{3}{5}$, what will $\frac{9}{11}$ of a yard cost?

Combination of E and the analysis of multiplication of parts.

NOTE.—The division analysis given in grade 7 are included in these, and form part of the grade. Give a thorough review of them before attempting the above combinations.

The following is the simplest form of the analysis of the important practical rule of "inverting the divisor," &c.

The introductory step of using a unit as the dividend is only a case of dividing one fraction by another.

Divide $\frac{2}{3}$ by $\frac{5}{7}$.

A unit divided by $\frac{5}{7}$, or $\frac{7}{7}\div\frac{5}{7}=\frac{7}{5}$, which is the divisor inverted; therefore $\frac{2}{3}$ of a unit divided by $\frac{5}{7}=\frac{2}{3}$ of $\frac{7}{5}=\frac{14}{15}$.

In the first step the unit is reduced to the same denomination as the divisor.

GEOGRAPHY.

"Geography of the United States in Detail."

1. In teaching the geography of the United States, it is particularly important that the time of the pupil be not exclusively taken up by the study of mere local details—by learning the several courses, &c., of long lists of rivers, and the exact situation of still longer lists of towns. A certain, but limited, amount of local geography is indispensable as a basis for the more important descriptive geography.

2. The necessary *local geography* embraces the names of the several States and Territories and their division into several groups, as New England, Middle, &c., &c.; their boundaries or relative positions; their important rivers, lakes, bays, capes, islands, mountain ranges, and peaks; the capital of each State, and a few of its other leading cities or towns, if of any importance. All these should be carefully learned as a basis for the subsequent portions of the study.

3. *The descriptive geography* should include the simplest physical outlines of the country as a whole; the *elevations*, the great mountain ranges, plateaux and plains; the *drainage* by single rivers on the Atlantic slope, and by extensive complex systems in the remainder of the country; the *climate*, with its modifications in the several sections, as cold or hot, wet or dry; the leading industries and staple agricultural, mineral, and manufactured productions, and their dependence upon the physical conditions.

4. Add to this a simple and very brief outline of the general and State governments, the population, its four races and their distribution; the great commercial routes, natural or artificial, and the cities, as the centres of manufacturing and commercial industry.

5. The descriptive geography of *individual States or Territories* may then, in great part at least, be deduced from a consideration of these general facts. All tiresome sameness and repetitions will thus be avoided, and the pupil will be made to appreciate the real importance of the study.

ELEMENTARY SCIENCE.

Botany.

1. The general suggestions given in connection with the subject of zoology, in the preceding grade, in relation to the extent of classification, the terms employed, &c., &c., are equally

applicable to the subject of botany. As a science of observation, this subject has a decided advantage over zoology, especially for educational purposes, inasmuch as the objects of which it treats are examined, dissected, and analyzed with more facility. They also possess more obvious beauty, and are devoid of the repulsiveness which attaches to so many objects of the animal kingdom. An insect, apparently disgusting at the first view, when closely examined, shows often more beautiful properties and more striking evidences of design than the most elegant blossom ; but the natural aversion to handle it or come in contact with it must first be overcome.

2. The *classification* of plants, being based upon distinctions often very minute, must, for the purposes designed to be accomplished in these simple lessons, be carefully limited. Common plants only need to be classified. The limitations of the classification to be taught are indicated below.

3. The first *few* lessons should show the *structure* of plants and the general functions of each of their parts,—the *root*, the *stem*, the *leaf*, the *flower*, the *seed;* the *growth* of the plant from the seed, both as to root and stem, the food of plants, buds and branches,—how a plant grows from them ; the distinction between *herbs*, *shrubs*, and *trees ;* also between *annuals*, *biennials*, and *perennials*. Examples of each to be given.

4. *Classification of leaves*—a beautiful and very useful department of the subject, especially as a means of training the powers of observation—may then be taught, the children being encouraged to gather specimens for careful scrutiny. The vocabulary employed to indicate the peculiarities is very interesting, and will serve to teach something of etymology—as *ovate*, *cordate*, *palmate*, *digitate*, *serrate*, &c., &c. Give the pupils *formulæ* for methodical examination and description. (See Miss Youmans' First Book of Botany.)

5. *Classification of roots and stems* to be taught in a similar manner, but much more briefly. Next, that of *blossoms*. First, show the parts of a blossom, taking a regular one to begin with

—as of a *lily*, a *morning-glory*, or a *butter-cup*. Analyze so that the pupils can see the parts, showing the *calyx* and *sepals*, the *corolla* and *petals*, the *stamens* and the *pistil with its ovary*. Give a sufficient number of exercises to make this familiar, and let the pupils analyze for themselves. The *principal forms* of flowers, as *bell-shaped*, *wheel-shaped*, *salver-shaped*, *cross-shaped*, *butterfly-shaped*, &c., &c., may then be shown. The *arrangement* of the blossoms on the stem (inflorescence), as far as it can be exemplified by actual specimens, as *head*, *raceme*, *spike*, *umbel*, &c., may also be learned.

6. The following outline of classification may be taught :—

A. (Series.) Flowering (*phœnogamous*) plants.

B. (Series.) Flowerless (*cryptogamous*) plants.

At first use only the *familiar* terms. The scientific may often be dispensed with entirely. Give examples of plants in each series ; as—

Rose, Lily, Geranium ;—Fern, Moss, Mushroom.

A, including *a* (class). Outside-growing (*exogenous*) plants.
b (class). Inside-growing (*endogenous*) plants.

Illustrate by *stems*, showing the rings or annual layers of growth in the former, with *bark*, *wood*, and *pith*, and their absence in the latter. Teach the coincident peculiarities of the leaves, as *netted-veined* and *parallel-veined*, affording a ready method (approximate) of distinguishing these plants, and thus giving opportunity for useful exercises ; also those of the seeds, as of two seed leaves (cotyledons), or only one, (*dicotyledonous* and *monocotyledonous*).

Familiar examples to be found by the pupils ; such as Rose, Buttercup, Geranium, Pea, Potato, Grape-vine, &c., &c., and Lily, Indian Corn, Common Grass, &c.

(*a*), Including 1. Orders or families of plants, with blossoms of many petals (*polypetalous*) ; and, 2. Orders, or families, of those, with blossoms of one petal (*monopetalous*). The pupils will readily find specimens of each, the names of which they have already learned.

The orders of (*b*) should not be taught. Nor need any instruction be given in relation to the classification of cryptogamous plants, *ferns, mosses*, &c., this being too difficult, and depending upon distinctions not sufficiently obvious for the purpose of these lessons. Attention, however, may, if occasion offers, be called to the *fructification* of ferns.

6. Such of the *orders*, or *families*, should be taught as are very familiar, and depend upon quite obvious distinctions, familiar names being exclusively used. Thus the *Mustard Family*, the *Pulse Family*, the *Crowfoot Family*, the *Rose Family*, the *Lily Family*, &c., &c., may be taught as far as the collection and presentation of specimens render it desirable; that is, not the mere fact that there are such families, but in connection with an actual object, and when the *inquiry* is, to what family does it belong? If the season permits, and there is an opportunity for the pupils to seek for specimens, this part of the instruction may be extended. Here the judgment of the teacher (never to be superseded) must be carefully exercised, it being constantly kept in view that the object of these lessons is not to make the pupils *botanists*, but to create a basis for the study of natural objects, and to develop the faculties of perception and reflection. *Species* need not be taught, although the pupils may, as occasion offers, be made to perceive the diversity presented by different individuals of the same family, so as to learn what is meant by species.

7. The *common uses of plants* may be taught to some extent incidentally with some of the above instruction, but more fully at this stage. This will embrace their uses for *food, clothing, medicine*, &c. Take our own plants first. Show that the *roots* of some plants are useful; of others, the *seeds;* others, the *leaves;* others, the *fruit;* others, the *bark*, &c. Some few plants of other climates and countries may then be referred to, as *cotton, rice, sugar, tea, coffee*, &c., &c. The relationship of these plants to our own may then be shown; that is, the *families* to which they belong.

FIFTH GRADE.

Outline Course.

Reading.—Of the grade of a Fourth Reader (first half), with the exercises of the preceding grades.

Spelling and Definitions.—From the reading lessons, as in the preceding grades.

Mental Arithmetic.—As far as in written arithmetic, with exercises as in the Sixth Grade.

Written Arithmetic.—Through decimals, with practical applications in both common and decimal fractions, and their conversion one into the other.

Geography.—Local and descriptive, through South America and Europe; the topics of the preceding grades to be occasionally reviewed in outline.

Elementary Science.—By oral instruction. The uses and qualities of familiar objects; also an outline knowledge of mineralogy, illustrated by specimens.

DIRECTIONS, &c.

Reading.—As in the preceding grades.

Spelling.—As in the *Sixth Grade.*

Definitions.— " " "

Mental Arithmetic.—General Directions, as in the *Seventh* and *Eighth Grades.*

(The character of the examples to be given to the pupils is suggested by the exercises in Written Arithmetic.)

Written Arithmetic.

1. Definitions pertaining to fractions should be retained and occasionally reviewed.

2. The exact nature of Decimal Fractions should be explained and illustrated; also the meaning of the word *decimal.* Show that Decimal Fractions may be used like Common Fractions by writing the denominator. Illustrate by the decimal notation, showing that whole numbers greater than 9 are also expressed *decimally.*

3. The illustrations may embrace the following :—1. How to write decimals, as 7-tenths, 7-hundredths, 7-thousandths, 7-ten-thousandths, &c.; 2. Show that the *numerator* is FIRST written, as in Common Fractions ; 3. Show that the " decimal point " and the ciphers, when used, are only required to *indicate* the *denominator* ; 4. In *reading* decimal fractions, the pupils should be cautioned to avoid such expressions as " tens of thousands" for *ten-thousandths* "hundreds of thousands," for *hundred-thousandths*, &c., &c. In connection with the reading of such fractions, pupils should be trained to recognize readily the comparative value of different fractions; as that .3 is greater than .0987, or .01 than .009596, &c. They may also be made to perceive readily the *approximate value* of decimals as compared with simple common fractions ; as, that .7634 is a little more than $\frac{3}{4}$; that .8741 is somewhat less than $\frac{7}{8}$, &c., Previous to this, however, it is well to teach the exact value of certain decimal expressions : as $.75=\frac{3}{4}$, $.125=\frac{1}{8}$, $.375=\frac{3}{8}$, &c., These exercises will serve to render the subsequent work of the pupil intelligible.

SYLLABUS OF TOPICS.

Exercises in READING decimal fractions.

Exercises in telling how many places are necessary for a given denominator, and *vice versa*.

Exercises in *writing* decimal fractions.

Reduction of decimal fractions:

1st. *By Inspection*, with analysis as in common fractions.
Examples, mental, oral, and written.

.3 to .00's, to .000's, &c. ; .15 to .00000's. Give analysis.

3 to .0's, to .00's, to .000's, &c. 7.3 to .0's, to .000's, &c.

Reduce .700 to *lowest* DECIMAL *terms*. Give analysis.

NOTE.—Avoid saying " the ciphers to the right are crossed off because they are of *no use*." The statement that " they do not affect the value," is not satisfactory unless the pupils show why they do not.

Reduce common fractions to decimal fractions. Give analysis.

Use axiom—$\frac{3}{4}$ of a unit$=\frac{1}{4}$ of 3 units; $\frac{3}{4}=\frac{1}{4}$ of 3.

Make this definite by objective illustration, using lines divided into parts.

$\frac{3}{4}$ to .0's, $\frac{3}{4}$ of $1=\frac{1}{4}$ of $3=\frac{1}{4}$ of 30 tenths$=7\frac{1}{2}$ tenths$=.7\frac{1}{2}=.75$.

NOTE.—Pupils should be accustomed to read decimal fractions, especially hundredths (in subsequent grades applied to per cent.), so as to include outstanding fractional parts, where there are any.

Example.—Reduce 4-11 to a decimal fraction of two places, or reduce 4-11 to hundredths.
Ans. Two places will give hundredths for the denominator.

$$\frac{4}{11} = \frac{1}{11} \text{ of } 4 = \frac{1}{11} \text{ of four hundred hundredths} = 11\overline{)4.00} \quad .36\ 4\text{-}11$$

$$\text{Reduce } \frac{240}{320} \text{ to a decimal: } \frac{240}{320} = \frac{24}{32} = \frac{3}{4} = \tfrac{1}{4} \text{ of } 3 = \tfrac{1}{4} \text{ of } 300 \text{ hundredths} = 4\overline{)3.00} \quad .75$$

Rule 1. 1st, Reduce the numerator to an improper fraction with the required denominator; 2d, Divide by the given denominator.

Rule 2. *Divide the numerator by the denominator.*

NOTE.—Give examples to show what common fractions in their lowest terms *can be made entirely decimal*, and which *can not* (*prima facie*, 2 *and* 5—contrasted with *all others*). In the general work of the class pupils should rarely be required to continue the division beyond three or four places.

Reducing Decimal Fractions to Common Fractions in their Lowest Terms.

Rule.—Write the fraction as a common fraction and reduce to lowest terms.

Examples: .625 .4125 .87500 14.125
" $.07\frac{1}{7}$ $.3\frac{1}{3}$ $.66\frac{2}{3}$ $5.11\frac{1}{9}$ $.87\frac{1}{2}$

NOTE.—Pupils should be made thoroughly familiar by rapid mental exercise, usually without analysis, with the decimal expressions for halves, 3ds, 4ths, 5ths, 6ths, 7ths, 8ths, 9ths, 11ths, 12ths, and *vice versa*, using preliminary reduction to lowest terms whenever possible, as in $\frac{9}{12}$, $\frac{6}{9}$, &c., &c.

Addition of Decimal Fractions.

Examples: Add .2, .05, .008, .7283. Add .0005, .97, .0101, &c.
" Give mixed numbers.

NOTE.—Explain, as in common fractions, by principle of lowest terms. The necessary additional ciphers may be "understood" in the solution, but not in the oral analysis, which should be *as brief as possible.*

Subtraction of Decimal Fractions.

Examples:—.1—.075; 1.001—.01009, &c.
Explain as in common fractions, with the same analysis.

Multiplication of Decimal Fractions.

NOTE.—Do not give large denominators; *use the brief rule of common fractions. Cases* as in common fractions:

1st. When a fraction or a mixed number is to be *multiplied*, as:
4 times .75, 17 times 8.047.
Value of 13 barrels at $8.375 a barrel.

2d. When a *fractional part* is to be taken, as:
.4 of .83, .4 of 75, .4 of 8.75.
How much is .7 of $38.45? .079 of $120? .90¼ of $160.48?
Value .179 of ton @ $92 a ton? at $92.87½ a ton?

3d. Combinations of the 1st and 2d cases, as:
3.4 lbs, at 79 cts. a lb.? $.79×3.4;
8 cwt., 75 lbs. @ $2.47 a cwt. $2.47×8.75.

NOTE.—As preliminary to 2d and 3d cases, give mental exercises in finding the *product* of two decimal denominators, as, 10ths by 10ths, how many places? 1000ths by 100ths, how many places? &c., &c.

Examples of cases involving reduction:

.024 × .15=? Product of numerators, 24 × 15=360, the new numerator, 1000ths by 100ths=100.000ths, or 5 decimal places for denominator. Ans. .00360=in lowest decimal terms, .0036. Why cross off the last 0? To divide both terms by 10.

NOTE.—Many questions are as well solved by the application of principle (G) in common fractions, 6th grade (see):
.079 of $14.83=.001 of 79 times $14.83, &c., &c.
Use or not, as may be judged expedient.

Division of Decimal Fractions.

There are two cases:

1st. When the divisor is *an integer*—
7÷8, 8÷7, 6÷5, 6÷120, 7.2÷6, 3.6÷120, &c. Put question in several ways: 1st, Divide, 7.2 by 6; 2d, How much is $\frac{1}{6}$ part of 7.2? 3d, How many times is 6 contained in 7.2? &c., &c.

This simple case does not require the principle of the common denominator.

2d. When the divisor is or contains a *decimal fraction:*
6.÷03, .8÷.005, .004÷.8, .0036÷.024, 7.2÷.009, 8.÷5.45, 3.÷7.203, .2÷8.75, .3006÷7.4, 8.5÷9.78, 8.638÷9.5, 8.638÷4.3, &c., &c.

Solution and analysis by the principle of common denominator.
There are two forms of applying this principle:

1st. Where the denominator of the divisor is the *greater*, (.003).6,) INCREASE the denominator of the dividend to .000's.

2d. Where the denominator of the divisor is the *less*, (.12).17286,) DIMINISH the denominator of the dividend to .00's by cutting off the last three figures.

A general rule: 1st, Reduce the denominator of the dividend to the denominator of the divisor; 2d, Divide one numerator by the other.

Applications.—The applications of decimal fractions will be principally found in Federal money. Simple combinations with common fractions should occasionally be made; also simple combinations of two or more of the rules of decimal fractions.

Use the principles of *cancellation* and *reduction to common fractions* whenever they will simplify the operation. It would be a *defect* in a class that had completed multiplication of decimal fractions, to go through the long process when finding .875 of a number. If properly taught, they will know the value of that fraction to be $\frac{7}{8}$, and will proceed accordingly.

Examples in finding what *decimal fraction* one decimal fraction is of another; especially how many *hundredths*—use ONLY small amounts or very simple examples:

8c., how many hundredths of 64c. ?

\$7.25, how many hundredths of \$9.75 ?

1st. What common fraction: $\frac{8}{64}=\frac{1}{8}=$? $\frac{725}{975}=\frac{29}{39}=$?

2d. What decimal fraction: $\frac{1}{8}=.125$ or $.12\frac{1}{2}$; $\frac{29}{39}=.74\frac{14}{39}$.

The last case is the extreme limit of "applications" in this grade, in which the example should *never* take the following involved form of statement: "Bought for \$9.75, sold at \$7.25 profit, how many hundredths did I gain?"

General Remarks.—It must not be forgotten that the teaching of *principles* and their most common and useful applications is the principal matter in the study of common and decimal fractions. Therefore AVOID LONG EXAMPLES.

Supplementary Note to the Arithmetic of the 7th, 6th, and 5th Grades.

Particular attention is directed to the three following elementary and mutually related problems, and to their importance as the essential preparation for the commercial arithmetic of the third and higher grades.

1st. To take a fractional part of a given number:

7th and 6th Grades.	*5th Grade.*	*3d Grade.*
How much are $\frac{3}{4}$ of 15?	How much are .75 of 15?	Find 75 per cent. of 15?
How much are $7\frac{1}{3}$ times $9\frac{1}{2}$?	How much are 3.48 times 7.53?	Find $62\frac{1}{2}$ per cent. of 8.75?
Value of $4\frac{2}{3}$ yards @ $\$5\frac{2}{7}$ a yard?	Value of 8.47 tons @ \$3.45 a ton?	Find $87\frac{1}{2}$ per cent. of $\$48.37\frac{1}{2}$?

2d. To find what (fractional) part one given number is of another given number:

6 is what com. fract. of 15?	6 is what dec. fract. of 15? 6 is how many 100th of 15?	6 is what per cent. of 15?
$7\frac{1}{3}$ is what com. fract. of $9\frac{1}{2}$?	$7\frac{1}{3}$ is what dec. fract. of $9\frac{1}{2}$? $7\frac{1}{3}$ is how many 100th of $9\frac{1}{2}$?	$7\frac{1}{3}$ is what per cent. of $9\frac{1}{2}$?
$\$4\frac{2}{3}$ are what com. fract. of $\$5\frac{1}{4}$?	$\$4\frac{2}{3}$ are what dec. fract. of $\$5\frac{1}{4}$? $\$4\frac{2}{3}$ are how many 100th of $\$5\frac{1}{4}$?	$\$4\frac{2}{3}$ are what per cent. of $\$5\frac{1}{4}$?

3d. To find the number of which a given number is a given fractional part:

85 is $\frac{5}{8}$ of what number?	85 is .625 of what number?	85 is $62\frac{1}{2}$ per cent. of what number?
$2\frac{1}{8}$ is $\frac{7}{9}$ of what number?	18.75 is 1.3 of what number?	or $8\frac{2}{3}$ / 8.45 is 11 per cent. of what number?
$\$8\frac{1}{7}$ are $\frac{4}{5}$ of what sum?	\$9.25 are 1.25 of what sum?	\$12.60 are $87\frac{1}{2}$ per cent. of what sum?

If these three principles are made reasonably prominent by simple practical examples in the 7th, 6th, and 5th grades, a large part of the time and labor of the teachers of the higher grades will be available for other equally important objects.

GEOGRAPHY.

SOUTH AMERICA.

1. *Local Geography.*—The Continent, as a whole, its boundaries, the names and relative positions, or boundaries, of its political divisions—a few of the chief capes and islands, the position and direction of the great plateaux and mountain ranges [use chalk sections roughly drawn on blackboard]—five or six of the most famous volcanoes. In the drainage, only two or three lakes, the courses of the Orinoco, the Amazon, the San Francisco, and the Parana described, and their great branches named and pointed out as systems, but not described.

The *local geography* of the several countries taken separately will be very brief, and will include a *review* of the matter previously considered in the study of the continent—that is, the relative positions or boundaries, the positions of the mountains and plateaux, the principal rivers, &c., &c., together with the capitals of the several countries, and about twenty-five of the other principal interior cities and seaports of the continent.

2. *Descriptive Geography.*—It will be found most expeditious and effective to teach first the descriptive geography of the continent as a whole. From this, that of the several countries may be very easily deduced and distinctly remembered. It should include the *surface* of the country as mountain, plateau, or plain—the *zones*—the *climate* as modified by latitude, elevation, and the prevalent winds—the leading characteristics of the great plains and plateaux—a brief notice of *volcanoes* and *earthquakes*—a few of the principal *plants* and *animals*—the three *races*, their distribution and principal occupations; the European *languages*—the chief *productions* and *exports*, vegetable, animal, and mineral, and the forms of *government.*

EUROPE.

The geography of Europe should be so taught as to avoid all minute detail. In *local geography* the boundaries of the continent, the names and relative positions or boundaries of its states; the position of its principal peninsulas, capes, gulfs, bays, seas, and straits; its chief highlands and lowlands; from twelve to fifteen principal mountain systems, the famous volcanoes, the great islands and groups of islands, seven or eight important lakes, including two or three in Switzerland; from twenty to twenty-five of the important rivers, specifying those which are important as commercial water-ways; the names and positions of the capitals of the several countries, and from fifty to seventy of the other important cities.

The descriptive geography to be on the same plan as for North and South America, avoiding long descriptions and long lists of places. It should include the general surface, climate, productions, peoples and their industries, together with their relations of blood, language, commerce, &c., with the people of the United States. In reviewing the chief cities, state any important or interesting facts in relation to each.

"*The topics of the preceding grades to be reviewed in outline.*"

This important requirement may best be met by making the exercise a comparative one. It should not be a home-lesson, but a vigorous class-room exercise, discarding the text-book and using the outline maps and the pointer. For instance, a rapid pointing out and naming of all the countries of America and Europe, and their capitals, might constitute one lesson; all the mountain systems, plateaux, plains, and volcanoes, another; the climate and productions, a third; and so on.

ELEMENTARY SCIENCE.

Mineralogy.

1. Read first the general remarks on teaching elementary science by oral instruction in the Eighth Grade.

2. In no other department is it so completely within the power of the teacher to present the subject to the *perceptions* of the pupils in the class-room. At the same time no one requires so

large a share of imparted information. This should not be given by the teacher until nothing more can be drawn from the pupils.

3. It is utterly impossible to teach the subject without *special preparation.* This preparation may be readily made with the assistance of *Dana's Manual of Mineralogy,* and *Day's Grammar School Cabinet,* or other similar text-books and appliances.

4. What has been said in preceding grades, as to the propriety or necessity of attempting only a part of the subject, is equally applicable here. What is done should be systematic—not miscellaneous and unrelated. Do not attempt to treat any topic exhaustively. A large part would not be understood or remembered, and valuable time would be misapplied.

5. The investigations made by the pupils in relation to each mineral should be guided by the teacher by means of a regular formula, considering in a fixed order its *form, structure, cleavage, fracture, hardness, weight, color, lustre, &c., &c.* These special characteristics and their proper order will be readily remembered after a little practice. Each term thus used should be carefully illustrated and explained as soon as its introduction becomes necessary.

6. Begin with *Minerals—Rocks* to be afterwards considered as mineral aggregates. A clear perception of the general properties of minerals may readily be given by commencing with ice—water—steam.

7. The pupil is then prepared to compare ice with a *quartz crystal,* which should be presented but *not at first named*—compared first as to the resemblances, then the differences. When the pupils can be made to furnish no more ideas, the teacher should state where it is found, its relative abundance, geological importance, economic uses, &c., &c. Be particular *not to introduce* an unexplained term—such as the NAME of any rock or mineral, as gneiss, or gypsum. The name means nothing until explained as quartz has been. Other forms of quartz may then follow, each treated in the same way, and each in its turn compared with those that have preceded it. This will constitute an excellent review, and will thoroughly fix what has been al-

already taught. Encourage the pupils to look for and bring in specimens which they think to be of the same character as those studied. *Let them tell* why they think they are the same. *Let others tell* why they think they are not.

8. Having thus treated of *quartz*, next consider, in the same way, *feldspar* and *mica*. The pupils will now be ready to consider a *rock*.

Let it be gneiss or granite. Let the pupils look for the minerals in it [a cheap single lens as a magnifier will often be of service]. Then consider the texture, structure, where found, uses, &c. The mineral *hornblende* and its important varieties may then follow, and after that the rock *syenite*.

All necessary information may be obtained from any of the Manuals in use.

9. It will not be necessary to follow out in detail all the minerals and rocks of which it is desirable that pupils have some knowledge. A list of the more important, mostly from Dana, is subjoined, from which the teacher will make such selections as will conform essentially to the above plan.

MINERALS.

Water, carbon, diamond, coal and coal-mining, anthracite, bituminous, jet, plnmbago, amber, petroleum, asphalt, sulphur, saltpetre, salt, borax, lime, gypsum, alabaster, selenite, calcite spar, chalk, stalagmites, limestones, crystalline and compact, marbles, quicklime, hydraulic lime, dolomite, alum, talc, soap-stone (French chalk), meerschaum, pyroxene and hornblende, corundrum and emery, feldspar, albite, orthoclase, garnet, mica.

METALS.

Mineralized [ores] or Native—Ores of tin, iron, nickel, zinc, lead, mercury, copper, gold, silver, platinum. Enter into no *details* of Metallurgy—a few simple facts in regard to smelting, fluxes, &c., will not be out of place. The economic uses of these metals and the poisonous properties of some of them should receive very careful attention.

ROCKS.

As single Minerals.—Example pure Limestone. As compounds—granite or conglomerate. Rocks as crystalline and uncrystalline, stratified and unstratified, aqueous, igneous and metamorphic.

The Relative Position of important Rocks.—Granite, syenite, gneiss, mica, slate, steatite, trap, basalt, lava, pumice, slate, shale, schist, quartzrock, burrstone, sandstones, grits, conglomorates, limestones, marbles, sand, clay.

Such of these rocks as are found on Manhattan Island, or in its vicinity, or have important uses in paving, flagging, building, &c., should receive particular attention.

CORRECTION OF LANGUAGE.

[For the Fifth, Sixth, Seventh, Eighth Grades.]

The prescribed course requires that "in all the grades the pupils shall be trained in the *correction of language*, and taught to avoid common errors of speech." This is to be accomplished in connection with the *dictation exercises* required in the several grades, also by oral exercises specially adapted to this purpose, and by *incidental instruction* during the recitations and lessons in other subjects, as in the definition exercises, the lessons in elementary science, &c. Indeed, every exercise in which the pupils are required to use their own language, either orally or in writing, should be made a vehicle for this instruction, the object being to impart the *habit of using correct language.* It is of the greatest importance that this habit should be acquired at an early age, for without it, the technical study of grammar will scarcely prove adequate to impart fluency in the correct use of language. The old habits, in spite of the knowledge of principles and rules, will be always apt to show themselves.

On this account, teachers cannot be too careful themselves in the use of language. Their *words* as well as their *acts* should present a model for the imitation of their pupils, and example in this, as in other things, will prove far more potent than precept. For special exercises in this department of the instruction, the following suggestions are made:

1. Write on the blackboard such faults in expression as are liable to be committed, including—1. Ungrammatical expressions: as *I haven't no book; I haven't got my pencil; I seen him do it*, &c. 2. Slang: *This is an awful easy lesson*, &c. The faulty expressions written in this way should, however, consist of such as may have been committed by some of the pupils of the class, lest those who have acquired good habits of speech be contaminated by having their attention called to such errors.

2. Award premium marks, or some other kind of reward, to those who succeed in pointing out improper expressions on the

part of their classmates; but let this be done in the right spirit, and not for the purpose of subjecting any of the pupils to jeers or ridicule. The fact that their language may be made the subject of criticism by their fellow-pupils, will put all on the alert to use the best modes of expression in their power, and then correction will have a permanent effect in improving them in the use of language.

3. Sometimes one or more pupils may be selected by the class to act as censors for a definite period (say a week), and to call attention to errors made by any of the pupils of the class. The object of this and the previous suggestion is to make the pupils critics on themselves and others, most of the inaccuracies committed resulting rather from carelessness and inattention than from a want of knowledge. The teacher will, of course, often find it necessary to give direct instruction in relation to certain expressions.

Of course no instruction in technical grammar, or in any grammatical rules, is required until the next grade.

FOURTH GRADE.

OUTLINE COURSE.

READING.—Of the grade of a Fourth Reader (latter half), with particular attention to emphasis, intonations, and naturalness of expression.

SPELLING AND DEFINITIONS.—As in the preceding grade.

MENTAL ARITHMETIC.—A review of the preceding grades, with exercises in calculation and analysis.

WRITTEN ARITHMETIC.—Through denominate numbers and fractions, with practical applications.

GEOGRAPHY.—Local and descriptive, through Asia, Africa and Oceanica; localities as in the preceding grades.

ENGLISH GRAMMAR.—To include the analysis, parsing and construction of simple sentences, and with such definitions *only* as pertain to the parts of the subject studied.

HISTORY OF THE UNITED STATES.—The early discoveries and the outlines of Colonial History to 1753; important events only to be taught, with such dates as are especially requisite for a complete understanding of the subject.

ELEMENTARY SCIENCE.—By oral instruction; the topics of the preceding grades continued and reviewed, and, in addition, the simple outlines of Physiology and Hygiene.

DIRECTIONS, &c.

READING.—1. In the preceding grades, due attention is required to be given to *emphasis* and *modulation;* but in this grade the exercises should take the *special* direction indicated by these departments of elocution, so as to lead to the higher stages of this art, required in the more advanced grades. It is not enough that the pupils should be accustomed to read with clear articulation and proper inflections of the voice; they should be taught *expression*—to comprehend the character of the piece read, to enter into its spirit, and, to some extent, at least, communicate it justly and forcibly.

2. *Vocal Culture.*—To accomplish this, the cultivation of the voice is requisite; and exercises should be employed with the

view to impart the *physical* as well as *mental* capabilities required for this purpose. The pupils should be taught the proper position of the body, and the right mode of using the lungs and the vocal organs so as to make their utterance effective. This kind of discipline has a most important bearing upon the general physical development of the pupils, as well as on the invigoration of the organs specially concerned in vocalization.

3. For the attainment of the special objects of this grade, the elocutionary rules, principles, and exercises contained in the Reader, should be made available; a portion of each reading-lesson being devoted to this kind of instruction and practice.

4. It is essential that the pupils should be required to stand while engaged in these exercises—either the whole class, or the particular pupil called upon to read. The other pupils, in a proper manner and in the right spirit, may be permitted to criticise the performance of the one called upon to read, and to exemplify the criticism by reading the same passage.

5. Lessons, especially such as involve a difficulty, should not be hurried over; they should be read and re-read, until an approximation, at least, to correctness has been attained by one or more pupils.

6. Concert reading and declamation may be resorted to occasionally, with very beneficial results.

Spelling and Definitions.—See suggestions in preceding grades.

ARITHMETIC.

Mental Arithmetic.—1. For the purpose of review, brief examples in fractions, both common and decimal, should be employed, so as to test, and more thoroughly fix in the pupil's mind, a knowledge of the principles and applications of fractions as taught in the preceding grades. The improvement made by the pupils in accuracy and rapidity, as well as in the ready application of arithmetical principles to particular cases, involving an exercise of the judgment, and reasoning powers, should be progressive from grade to grade, and therefore should be carefully tested in the mental work.

2. The *special* province of this grade being *Denominate Numbers*, the exercises should deal largely with the applications of fractions to that class of numbers, including Federal money, and should, of course, combine practice in all the essential tables of weight, measure, &c.

3. The teacher need not, perhaps should not, conform himself to the order or kind of examples presented by any particular text-book. If the questions given out to the pupils to be solved *instanter*, are spontaneously constructed by the teacher, they will be more appropriate to the special needs of the pupils, and the exercise will have far more spirit, and be of far greater value. It is among the dullest of all the occupations of the class-room to read from a book questions in mental arithmetic, of little variety, hackneyed in form and character, and which the pupils have previously been required to con over. To expect an uninterested, drowsy class to perform any intellectual exercise, is absurd; but the absurdity is greater, perhaps, in mental arithmetic than in any other subject.

4. The review of the analysis previously taught, should be systematic and thorough, but should not consume a large part of the time of the pupils.

WRITTEN ARITHMETIC.—1. The arithmetic specially prescribed in this grade, both mental and written, is of a practical character, perhaps more generally so than in any of the other grades of the course. All that precedes has been, to a considerable extent, a preparation for the work of this grade, and will be found involved in it. In view of the great importance of the subject, and in order to render the requirements as definite as possible, the syllabus given below presents, 1st. Certain preliminary considerations; and, 2d. Specific directions as to the extent of the field comprehended in the grade.

2. The whole subject of compound denominate numbers is strictly *utilitarian*. Practical utility should, therefore, be the controlling element in all the exercises employed. The daily necessities of the house, the shop, the market, &c., indicate the general character of the selections to be made. These will

furnish at least as good mental discipline in calculation and analysis as those of a less severely practical character.

3. The average time which pupils in this grade can yet spend in school is short. Secure, therefore, the essentials first. Review and test thoroughly the indispensable basis—the tables. (See Grades 8 and 7.) Train your pupils to work with reasonable rapidity. Carefully avoid long and complex examples. Avoid all things obsolete or obsolescent. Keep a clear record of the points you have covered. It will assist in the reviews and in the examinations. Do not dwell so long on Reduction as to omit important practical points in other rules. With the tables commence Reduction. See that the tables are not only memorized but understood.

SYLLABUS.

Reduction Descending.—Why so called—Denominations always written—Do not allow pupils to "add in" by a separate line; it greatly increases the work and the time and indicates mental feebleness. Explain by any process which makes the multiplier an abstract number. When the question will allow it, insert frequently the finding of the value at a given price.

Reduction Ascending.—Best taught and understood in immediate connection with Reduction Descending, at first by reviewing the same example. Do not allow long division by divisors less than 13, nor if cutting off 0's will change to short division.

Explain by any process which will clearly account for the denominations of the successive quotients and remainders.

The necessary analyses have already been given in the preceding grades. The "adding in" is identical with that in the reduction of mixed numbers.

Weights.—Teach briefly by examples the relations of Avoirdupois and Troy weights, the essential identity of Troy and Apothecaries' weights. Let most of the examples in Reduction be in the first of the three. They should be few and very short in the last.

Remember that the quarter of a hundredweight is seldom used now excepting in text-books—the Avoirdupois dram nowhere else.

In addition and subtraction give only avoirdupois weight. Remember that in things sold by the ton, the ounce is not taken into account. Review the principle of carrying if that plan is used—of its better substitute if not. A short question in Troy weight may be written upon the board or read from the text-book if pupils have one. Then require them *to state succinctly* what process will be required in working it, omitting detailed analysis.

NOTE.—To avoid repetition, it may here be stated, that the plan just mentioned may be taken in multiplication and division as well as in reduction, addition, and subtraction, with those portions of the weights, measures, &c., practice in which is of less general utility. Many practical examples in multiplication and division will arise under Avoirdupois weight, such as finding values at so much a pound, hundredweight or ton, or *vice versa*. Such examples may involve preliminary addition or subtraction, or both.

Linear Measure.—Reduction.—Employ the denominations most in use—the inch, the foot, the yard, the rod, and the mile—very rarely, if ever, all in the same example. Omit cloth measure, or if briefly referred to, use only $\frac{1}{2}$s, $\frac{1}{4}$s, $\frac{1}{8}$ths and $\frac{1}{16}$ths. Give a very few examples to show the use of the chain and its subdivisions. Measuring tapes usually have feet on one side and chains and links on the other. One may be employed to advantage in the class-room. To convert feet or yards into miles, and *vice versa*, use only 5,280 and 1,760; so many miles of railroad track, so many lbs. of iron to yard at so much a ton, &c., &c. Omit addition and subtraction, multiplication and division.

Surface Measure.—(*Of very great practical importance.*)—Treat briefly in reduction. Be particular to avoid long examples. When 30¼ is used as a divisor let it be in very short examples. Give examples in addition and subtraction. In multiplication and division give examples in finding areas of rectangular figures, in feet, in yards, &c. Give the feet, or the chains, on the sides of rectangles to find acres and value; acres and hundredths the most usual form. Omit roods. Simple questions may be given occasionally, involving cost, in plastering, bricks, carpeting rooms, dress linings, &c., &c.; also very simple questions in finding area, circumference or diameter of circle *when square root is not involved*, using $\frac{22}{7}$ or 3.1416 and .7854 for ratio.

Solid Measure.—Employ only the inch, the foot, the yard, and the cord; use the last but little. See that pupils understand the mutual relations of linear, surface, and solid measures, and that they are not convertible, the units being of totally different natures. Reduction—a few simple questions. Omit addition and subtraction. Give examples in finding cubic inches, feet or yards in boxes, bins, cellars, cylindrical cisterns, &c., &c. Some knowledge of *board measure*, giving very simple practical examples involving cost.

Dry and Liquid Measures.—Use no obsolete denominations. Omit beer measure. Remember that the barrel and the hogshead are not often measures in commerce. Simple examples in reduction. Omit addition and subtraction. Give the simplest possible examples, in connection with solid measure, in finding bushels or gallons in bins, vats, cisterns, &c., using 231 and 2150 cubic inches, and omitting fractions. No other multiplication or division is required.

Circular Measure.—Treat briefly; explain the terms and their use; omit signs. Reduction—Short examples of two or three terms. Addition and Subtraction—Questions in difference of latitude and longitude. Geographical and statute miles on the meridian, on the equator, on parallels of 60°.

Time.—(In part very important.) Treat reductions very briefly. Do not involve more than two or three denominations in one example. Leap-year. Addition and subtraction. Difference of dates—By days, by years, months and days. Relations of difference of longitudes to time. Explanations and examples. Conversion of longitude into time and *vice versa.*

Miscellaneous.—Practical examples in values, involving dozen, gross, quire, ream, quintal, barrels of flour, fish, &c., making out simple bills, receipts, &c.

Money.—Reduction and other simple exercises in Federal money are always in order from the Eighth Grade. Give but few examples in each rule in sterling money. Reduction of sterling to Federal and *vice versa,* omitting, of course, all reference to the percentage of exchange.

Pupils should know something of the money of Canada—identical with our own—the value of the franc, and the dollar of the Zollverein.

Fractional Compound Numbers.—The consideration of this subject has been deferred to avoid complicating it with simpler and more important matters. Reject all examples in addition, subtraction, multiplication, and division. In reduction *there are but two cases,* and the second of these is simply the converse of the first. Each divides into two varieties, in one of which the fraction is common and in the other decimal, but the principle applied in working is the same.

Be careful to select only those denominate numbers in which such fractional quantities are likely to need consideration, chiefly sterling money.

Examples: Case 1st. A. $\frac{33}{77}$ of a bushel to pecks, quarts, &c.
B. .673 of a £, how many shillings, pence, &c., or dollars and cents.

" Case 2d. A. 7 ft. 95 in., what common fraction of a cubic yard?
B. 15 cwt. 38 lbs. are what decimal fraction of a ton?
£8 14s. 9½d. are how many dollars and cents (at $4.84)?

GEOGRAPHY.

1. Complete the local and descriptive geography of one continent or grand division before beginning that of another.

2. The same general plan should be pursued as in the Sixth and Fifth Grades. If the simple physical features of Asia, for instance, be first taught as a whole, including the climate, with the use of the pointer and the outline map to expedite the process, the descriptive geography of the individual countries will involve but little labor, and will be easily remembered.

3. The geography of Asia is by far the most important and interesting. The geography of Africa and Oceanica is comparatively simple, and should be reduced, in teaching, to the nar-

rowest limits that will give a clear view of the general physical conditions of surface and climate, and of the social conditions of the various races, together with a knowledge of the leading productions and exports, and the location of the principal cities. One of the most comprehensive and important elements of a general review is, to show the relations of Europe to all the other grand divisions of the globe as to conquest, settlement, colony, language, &c. This may be taught in a very brief and general way, and is indispensable to a correct outline knowledge of the present condition of the human race,—one of the great objects of the study of geography.

GRAMMAR.

The instruction in this subject required for the 4th grade includes *analysis*, *parsing*, and *construction*, and in the order mentioned. Grammar is the *science of the sentence ;* and, therefore, the fundamental idea to be imparted is, *what constitutes a sentence.* Oral lessons should precede the study of the text-book, as a preparation for it. The ideas involved in the *definitions* should first be developed, before the pupils are required to commit these definitions to memory. The contrary practice, once so common, is very discouraging and injurious to the pupil, since it compels him to learn by rote a mass of verbiage which is perfectly unintelligible to him.

Let a short sentence be written on the slate or blackboard; and then by analysis, let the pupils be made familiar with the relations of the words used as *subject*, *verb* or *predicate*, and *adjuncts*. The distinctions comprehended in the *parts of speech* can all be successively taught in this way, and the pupil enabled readily to point them out, before he is required to say what a noun, or pronoun, or verb, &c., is. The learning of the definitions will be easily accomplished as he proceeds.

The object of the *analysis* is to find out in what relation the words used in the sentence stand to one another (general grammar) ; the object of the *parsing* (only another kind of analysis) is to apply the principles and rules proper to these relations (particular grammar) ; the object of the *construction* is to impart practical skill in applying these rules and principles, as well as to give thereby clearer ideas of their nature and use.

Thus, when the teacher presents the sentence, "Industrious pupils learn very rapidly," the pupil is made to discover, first, the principal parts—*subject* and *verb*, or *simple predicate*; next, that *industrious* is added to *pupils*, *rapidly* to *learn*, and *very* to *rapidly*. The pupil then knows that *industrious* being an adjunct of a noun is an adjective; that *rapidly* being an adjunct of a verb, is an adverb, and that *very* being an adjunct of an adverb is also an adverb. This instruction can be supplemented by requiring the pupils to construct sentences of a similar kind; as, sentences containing a simple subject and predicate,—sentences containing a subject and adjuncts with a simple predicate,—sentences containing a subject and predicate, with adjuncts of both. Some of these sentences may be required to be *declarative*, some *interrogative*, &c. In this way the ingenuity or invention of the pupil is brought into play in connection with his knowledge of grammar; and the exercises glide progressively into extended composition.

The sentences presented should at first be carefully classified so that no difficulties may be presented which are beyond the pupils' ability or actual attainments to solve. In grammar, especially, should the instruction be systematic and logical.

Etymological exercises should be interspersed, especially in the use of the *apostrophe* as the sign of the possessive case—in the proper plural termination of nouns—the proper forms of the pronouns, &c. This is a point of considerable importance.

The sentences required to be studied in this grade include,

1. Sentences with a simple subject and a simple predicate; 2. Those with simple word adjuncts of either subject or predicate or both; 3. Those with simple phrase adjuncts (so as to teach the *preposition*); 4. Those with compound subjects or compound predicates, or both, but of an easy character; as, John, William, and Samuel are diligent boys,"—"The animals turned, looked, and ran away." This class of sentences will serve to introduce the *conjunction*.

1. It is especially requisite in all the lessons given on this subject that the instruction should not be allowed to degenerate into the repetition of formulæ, and instead of being made a

means of developing the analytic and reasoning faculties of the pupils, become a piece of worse than useless mechanism. Grammatical instruction has a distinct office as an educational agent,—an office that can be performed by no other subject. It is addressed to faculties that probably cannot be trained in any other way; and, therefore, no educational curriculum would be complete without it. It must, however, be carefully kept within proper limits, both as to time and place; and must not be permitted to encroach upon other branches of equal importance. Each department of it must also have its due share of attention.

Of course the study of grammar as prescribed in this grade does not supersede the "exercises for correction," required in all the grades. These exercises, however, by degrees lose their *empirical* character and become scientific.

HISTORY OF THE UNITED STATES.

General Suggestions.—1. The *leading purpose* of this study is that the pupil may understand the origin, character and condition of the nation of which he is a part, and that he may be fitted for an intelligent exercise of his duties and responsibilities as a citizen.

2. It is obviously impossible to treat so comprehensive a subject exhaustively. The immaturity of the pupil's mind and the pressure of other studies alike forbid. Yet the leading facts and principles may be readily comprehended and remembered, and the outline which he is to retain be made from the first coherent and definite.

3. To this end a simple *preliminary outline sketch* should be carefully fixed in the minds of the pupils of the Fourth Grade, and frequently reverted to in the reviews of all the grades in which the subject is taught. The geography already learned will greatly simplify the process. This outline can be given most expeditiously and efficiently by means of oral instruction and the use of the map. It should be very brief, and, if it is

expedient, be reduced to writing by the pupil for reference. All detail should be reserved for the study of the text-book.

The following sketch is presented only as illustrative of this suggestion. Its modification by rearrangement or otherwise, or the substitution of another in its place, is left entirely to the discretion of the principal.

OUTLINE SKETCH.

1st. The people of the United States are of European descent, excepting the negroes.

2d. Less than 400 years ago our ancestors knew nothing of the existence of this Continent.

3d. Spain, guided by Italian genius, led the way to its discovery, exploration, and colonization.

4th. The first permanent English settlement within our limits was not effected until more than a century after the voyage of Columbus. In the interval, Spain and Portugal had possessed themselves of the shores and islands of the Mexican Gulf and of nearly all South America.

5th. For a century and a half the English colonies were confined to a narrow strip east of the Alleghanies.

6th. Spanish slavery exterminated the Indians of the West Indies. This led directly to the opening of the African slave trade, and indirectly to the introduction of slaves into our own country.

7th. The colonies had wars with the Indians in whose country they had settled and with the neighboring French colonies. The French were subjugated and their territories occupied.

8th. Less than a century ago all European settlements were yet dependent colonies.

9th. The necessities of distant colonial settlements had developed in the English colonies a spirit of self-reliance and political freedom and a system of local and elective self-government.

10th. The expenses of the French wars left a heavy debt and led to unusual taxation. A tyrannical system of taxation led to the War of Independence, which fixed the national boundary at the Mississippi. The colonies had become States.

11th. The present form of government (the Constitution) was established soon after the close of the war, about eighty-three years ago.

12th. The number of States has been greatly increased by immigration and emigration. The population and wealth have increased many fold.

13th. By purchase and otherwise the national territory has been expanded to the Gulf of Mexico and to the Pacific and Arctic oceans.

14th. Since the War of Independence there have been three important wars: 1. A *war with England* in defence of naturalized citizens and in vindication of the rights of neutrals; 2. A *war with Mexico*, resulting from our annexation of Texas; 3. A *great civil war*, arising in part from questions originating in our colonial history and in part from more recent causes.

Lessons and Recitations.—1. Lessons should be assigned by topics and not by pages.

2. All verbatim recitations of sentences and paragraphs should be strictly forbidden, and the pupils be required to state the facts in their own language.

3. Only such dates should be committed to memory as are indispensable as landmarks in history. The *sequence* of events, rather than the precise date of each, is what is usually necessary.

4. Maps, especially those of the text-books, should be used whenever the subject requires it.

5. Historic episodes, however interesting, should not receive the careful study given to the essential narrative. The stories of Juan Ponce de Leon, the Conquest of Mexico, De Soto's Expedition, John Smith, Pocahontas, the Salem Witchcraft, &c., &c., should indeed be carefully read, and, as far as may be necessary,. explained; but, unless great care is taken by the teacher, the pupils will be apt to conceive that these are the most important portions of the history.

6. Important incidental allusions to European history, such as the rise of the English Puritans, the expulsion of the Stuarts, the French Revolution, &c., should be carefully but briefly explained. Great caution must be exercised throughout to state all facts in such a manner as not to wound the religious or political sensibilities of any.

Reviews.—Reviews of the portion already taught, with frequent references to the preliminary sketch, are of the highest importance. These reviews should take three distinct forms: the *Chronological*, the method usually followed in the text-book; the *Biographical*, requiring the pupil to state all that has been learned in regard to particular individuals, and the *Geographical*, requiring a statement of all important facts relating to the history of a locality. Many of the topics treated by the second and third of these methods necessarily become cumulative. For instance, the facts relating directly to Washington will be gathered from at least three distinct and important periods in our history. A connected statement of the important events that have taken place in Philadelphia, or in the valleys of the Hudson and Lake Champlain, or in the State of Virginia, will necessarily cover a large part of the general subject in the higher grades. Such statements must be, of course, brief, and frequently will be mere chronological synopses.

Many of these reviews and certain parts of the regular recitations may be made spirited general exercises for the whole class by the use of the slate or paper. The writing of the few essential dates, the sequence of important events, the names of important individuals, &c., &c., are instances. The narrative reviews will necessarily be for the most part oral.

It will be observed that the system of reviews above suggested must, if faithfully carried out, result in a thorough unifying of the general subject in the mind of the pupil.

Suggestions for the Fourth Grade.

The essential points requiring careful study and frequent review in the history assigned to this grade are given below. Other interesting facts usually stated in text-books should be carefully read, but should receive a less proportionate share of attention. In no other grade is frequent reference to the maps so important.

Syllabus of Topics.

Voyage of Columbus—the naming of America—the occupation by the Spaniards of the West India islands and all the neighboring portions of the Continent—their enslavement of the Indians and its results (the last very briefly).

The discovery, exploration, and occupation of the St. Lawrence and Nova Scotia by the French.

Virginia.—The settlement of Jamestown and the events directly leading to it. The cultivation of tobacco—the introduction of slavery—the navigation acts and Bacon's rebellion.

Maryland.—The Calverts—religious freedom—Clayborne.

New England.—The Plymouth Company and the settlements under their patent. The Puritans—their previous history—why called Pilgrims. Settlement of Plymouth—of Boston—of Dover—Massachusetts Bay Colony. Settlement of Connecticut—of Rhode Island—provisions for religious freedom. The Union—Indian Wars (read)—Andros, King William's War, its causes and results. Salem Witchcraft (read). Queen Anne's War, its causes and results—King George's War, its causes and results.

New Netherlands.—Hudson—Settlement on the Delaware—at Fort Orange—at Manhattan Island—the Dutch Governors—Kieft's conduct—Stuyvesant—Existing evidences of the Dutch occupation.

New York.—Changes of name—reconquest by the Dutch and restoration to England. Andros—the extent of his rule. Dongan—Leisler—Schenectady—the Negro plot—Existing evidences of English rule.

New Jersey.—Its name—its division—union with New York—separation.

Delaware.—Settlement by Swedes—conquest by Stuyvesant.

Pennsylvania.—William Penn—his grant—his objects. Settlement of Philadelphia—relations to Delaware.

North Carolina.—The grant of Charles II—its limits—John Locke.

South Carolina.—Charleston settled—Carolina divided into two separate governments, 1729.

Georgia.—Savannah settled—character of Oglethorpe.

General condition of the English colonies in 1752. Their population—their national derivation, their industries, social condition, planters, patroons, proprietors—the causes which were developing a love of liberty.

Review *Chronologically* under heads of sovereigns of England—Elizabeth—James I—Charles I—Cromwell—Charles II—James II—William and Mary—Anne—George I—George II.

Review *Biographically.*

Physiology and Hygiene.

1. The chief purpose of this study in the Grammar Schools is, to give useful practical knowledge of the laws of health. As this subject receives, at most, but a small part of the time of a single grade, it is the more important that only those parts of it should be considered that are essential to the main purpose.

2. The teacher will observe that Anatomy, which occupies so much space in many text-books, is not called for in this grade, except as far as it is necessary to teach what is specially prescribed. It is a matter of little consequence to the pupil to know exactly the number of bones, or vertebræ, or pairs of muscles in his body, or to repeat their scientific names. Only those anatomical terms and facts should be introduced that are inseparable from the main subject (*physiology and hygiene*).

3. *Oral description* of structure or function should take the place of *definitions.* These may be omitted altogether.

4. The appliances necessary for teaching this branch are, the blackboard and charts. The teacher should carefully consider, at every step, to what extent the subject can be treated objectively. This can in part be done by drawing the pupil's attention to his own body, as in case of the pulse, the veins, arteries, respiration, etc. For several very important parts of the subject, there is no better apparatus than that which can be procured without expense at any butcher's stall, such as the lungs and windpipe of a sheep; the diaphragm, the heart and part of the great tubes leading to and from it; the brain and the bony cavity which contains it; the eye; portions of the spinal cord and nerves; small glands; and portions of limbs showing the relations of muscles, tendons, ligaments and joints. None of these need present anything offensive or disgusting. Add to these a small knife, and proper preparation on the part of the teacher, and the instruction given will be both interesting and profitable. Where it would not be expedient to resort to this means of illustration, preparations (similar to those manufactured by Auzout) could be used, when supplied by the Board to the schools, and in their absence, diagrams and charts.

5. A *syllabus* of leading points is subjoined. It is not required that all these should be taught in one class, though all are important. Neither is it expected that any point shall be treated exhaustively, nor is the teacher obliged to follow exactly the order laid down. Any order (so that it be an *order*) which presents the parts of the subject taught in their natural relations, will be satisfactory.

SYLLABUS OF TOPICS.

The pupil should be led to look upon the body as a complex apparatus for the use of his mind. To know that it consists primarily of—

First, a bony frame-work (the skeleton); *Second,* a motor apparatus attached to the frame (the muscular system); *Third,* a directing apparatus by which the mind controls the body (brain and nervous system, and sensory organs); *Fourth,* a general envelope protecting the preceding, as well as serving other purposes of the skin.

He should then be led to see that every motion of the body or of its minutest part, however slight and whether voluntary or involuntary, requires the *destruction* of a minute part of the organism and the removal of the destroyed part from the system,—that this constant destruction and removal make necessary a corresponding *reconstruction* and *renewal*, by means of new material, and that for these purposes there are provided—

Fifth, a circulatory apparatus,—(the blood-vessels)—to carry away old material and to distribute the new; *Sixth*, an aerating apparatus (the respiratory system), to purify, warm and enliven the circulating fluid; *Seventh*, a system of drainage (the skin and kidneys), to take from the blood a large part of the worn-out material; and *Eighth*, an apparatus to prepare and supply the new material (the digestive and assimilative organs).

8. Under each of these heads a few points are noted:

1. *Bones*,—their composition and various uses; *joints* and their lubrication;—important peculiarities of the spinal column; cautions as to injuring the large bones of an infant; the repairs of broken bones.

2. *Muscles and Tendons*,—their uses,—their arrangement in pairs, and why; how attached, how able to contract; effects of exercises; use of calisthenics.

3. *Nervous System*,—means of becoming conscious of the external world;—spinal cord,—its importance and protection, its ramifications,—effects of severing or injuring the spinal coard; care of infants in this respect. The sympathetic system, the nerves (as telegraph wires), the brain and its principal functions; uses of pain,—uses of sleep,—excitement, caution against,—late hours, stimulants, etc.

Special Senses,—touch, papillae,—taste,—smell;—the ear, its mechanism, hearing;—the eye, its mechanism, sight,—abuse of the eye.

4. *Skin*,—its structure and uses. Perspiratory glands and tubes,—uses of perspiration,—importance of bathing,—of proper clothing,—sympathy of skin with lungs—with digestive organs,—caution against exposure of limbs, arms or chests of little children; the skin as an absorbent;—danger of cosmetics and hair-dyes; treatment of burns and scalds, etc.

5. *Circulation*,—general relations of heart, arteries, veins and capillaries,—valves—pulsc—its rate—rapidity of circulation. Effects of fresh air and exercise on the circulation; limits of exercise,—dangers of excessive rope-jumping, etc. Effects of sleep, cautions necessary;—effects of tight garments—of scanty garments,—of insufficient or improper food,—wounds,—how to know when an artery is wounded, and what to do.

6. *Respiration*.—Practically the most important department of hygienic knowledge. The apparatus,—how protected—arrangement of ribs for flexibility, and the expansion of the lungs—muscles of chest and diaphragm concerned in respiration; importance of the diaphragm; show its positions at beginning and end of inspiration; the trachea; the organ of the voice,—minute structure of lungs—the cells and their membrane—exosmosis and endosmosis simply stated; intimate relations of capillaries and air-vessels; frequent full inspiration a means of increasing the capacity of the lungs; pernicious effects of tight lacing on the capacity and action of the lungs. The air—its composition—relations of oxygen to carbon and hydrogen introduced with food—products of respiration all invisible except

water—poisonous nature of carbonic acid—in wells—in vats—effects of smaller quantities, many other things thrown off by lungs and skin—effects of tobacco, liquor, carious teeth, etc., etc. Rapid diffusion of gases and vapors- ventilation of class-rooms,—of sleeping-rooms,—devices for ventilation of small sleeping-rooms in winter—why called "*vital air*"—careful inspection of premises to remove all decomposing substances, etc.; foul air from cellars, sewers, sinks, water-pipes, garbage, gas-lights, stoves, etc.; simple and cheap disinfectants—chloride of lime—chlorine—sulp. of iron—carbolic acid, etc. Respiration as affected by position, in standing—in sitting—especially in sitting to write—drawing. Popular errors in regard to condition of drowned persons—proper treatment for their resuscitation.

7. The digestive apparatus—the teeth, their uses, structure and hygiene—brief notice of salivary glands, their position and uses,—of the gullet—structure and function of the stomach—brief notice of the duodenum, the intestines, lacteals, etc.,—importance of the liver—the link between the digestivc and the circulatory systems. Dyspepsia, its preventable causes and terrible consequences—importance of chewing the food,—of regular hours in eating,—of light suppers—of good cooking—the art of preparing wholesome food the most important of household arts—common errors to be avoided in the preparation of food—common poisons and their antidotes.

THIRD GRADE.

OUTLINE COURSE.

Reading.—Of the grade of a Fourth Reader, continued, with exercises as in the preceding grades.

Spelling.—From the reading lessons, with exercises in writing miscellaneous words and sentences, and in the analysis and construction of words, according to the rules for spelling. *Definitions* from the reading lessons.

Mental and Written Arithmetic.—Commercial, through percentage, interest, and profit and loss. Problems to be chiefly such as involve the ordinary business transactions.

English Grammar.—Continued, with the analysis, parsing, and construction of easy complex and compound sentences; also, writing short compositions under the inspection of the teacher.

History of the United States.—From 1753 to 1789; the outlines of the Revolutionary War to be taught, and the events which led to the adoption of the Constitution.

Natural Philosophy.—Including Mechanics, Hydrostatics, and Pneumatics. A simple text-book to be used.

DIRECTIONS, &c.

READING.—See suggestions in the Fourth Grade.

SPELLING.—1. Oral spelling, except for the purpose of teaching *syllabication*, should be discontinued. The proper division of words into syllables is an important matter, and should receive due attention. In this connection the correct use of the *hyphen* in compounds should be taught, and the pupils exercised therein.

2. The *written exercises* should be correctly performed, with care not only as to penmanship, but as to capitals, punctuation, &c. These exercises should be carefully inspected, and, after the errors have been pointed out, should be revised and corrected by the pupil. The sentences used for dictation should contain a sufficient number of *common test words*, including proper names, both of persons and places, so as to impress the orthography of such terms firmly on the pupils' minds.

ARITHMETIC.

1. The commercial arithmetic of this grade differs from that taught in the preceding grades, chiefly in the introduction of the various forms of percentage.

2. The divisions of this subject should be presented in the following order: First, *simple percentage*, in four cases—one fundamental and three derived; second, the *applications* of simple percentage, technically known as *Profit and Loss*, following the same order and with the same analysis as in the four cases of simple percentage.

Those who prefer to do so may combine these divisions under the general head of "percentage not involving time."

The third division of the subject is *interest*, or "percentage involving time." It has five cases—one fundamental and four derived.

3. In treating this subject many skillful teachers prefer to introduce algebraic formulæ, in which the initial letters of the several terms employed in percentage are the elements. To this course there is no objection, *provided* that the formulæ be not employed in the mental arithmetic, and that they accompany the usual *analysis* and be not used as a *substitute* for it. With this exception, the processes and explanations of the mental arithmetic should not differ from those of the written arithmetic, the chief distinction between the two being that in the latter the numbers are too large to be carried in the mind.

4. The subject of arithmetic being necessarily and to a great extent cumulative, the teacher of the Third Grade is especially advised to read over the directions given in all the preceding grades, and in particular the table on page 96. For the sake of brevity, the terms base, percentage, &c., are employed in the following syllabus of topics in the usual technical sense of the text books. The teacher will so use them or not, as the principal may deem expedient.

Syllabus of Topics.

The term *percentage*—Reading per cents.

Examples—Read the following decimal fractions as per cents: .75, .8, .605, .003, .08½, .00¾, &c., &c.

Change common fractions to per cents. and *vice versa:*

Examples—$\frac{3}{4}$, $\frac{7}{8}$, $\frac{450}{900}$, $\frac{33}{88}$, $2\frac{4}{5}$, $1\frac{2}{11}$, $\frac{13}{17}$, &c., &c.

" 25 per cent., 75 per cent., $33\frac{1}{3}$ per cent., $14\frac{2}{7}$ per cent., $88\frac{8}{9}$ per cent., $325\frac{7}{8}$ per cent., $137\frac{1}{2}$ per cent., &c., &c.

NOTE—The common business fractions, halves, thirds, &c., to twelfths, inclusive, should be reduced to per cents., and the pupils made thoroughly familiar with them.

1ST CASE (*Fundamental*).

To find the *percentage*, the *base* and rate *being* given.

See table, page 96.—To find a given fractional part of a given number.

Examples—How much is 9 per cent. of 750? Had $750 in the bank; drew out 9 per cent. How much was it?

Analysis as in the multiplication of decimal fractions.

NOTE—When this form of the case has been taught, its *modifications* should immediately follow.

Examples—Had $750; paid out 9 per cent. How much had I left?

" Had $750; earned 9 per cent. more. How much had I then?

2D CASE (*Derived*).

To find the *rate* when the *percentage* and *base* are given.

See table, page 96.—To find what fraction one given number is of another given number.

Examples—140 is what per cent. of 400?

" Had 400 sheep; sold 140. What per cent. did I sell?

Analysis as in reducing a common fraction to a decimal fraction whose denominator is hundredths.

Modifications of Case 2d:

Examples—I had 400 sheep; I now have 540. What is the per cent. of increase?

Examples—I had 400 sheep; I now have only 260. What is the per cent. of decrease? or what per cent. have I left?

3D CASE (*Derived*).

To find the *base* when the *percentage* and *rate* are given.

See table, page 96.—To find the number of which another number is a given fraction.

Examples—140 is 35 per cent. of what number?

" Sold 140 sheep, which was 35 per cent. of my flock. How many had I at first?

Analysis as in simple fractions—140 is $\frac{35}{100}$ of what number?

Modifications of Case 3d:

Example—Sold 140 sheep, which was 35 per cent. of my flock. How many had I left?

Example—Sold 140 sheep, and have 65 per cent. of my flock remaining. How many had I at first?

4TH CASE (*Derived*).

To find the *base* when the *amount* (or difference) and *rate* are given.

To find a number which differs by a given fractional part of itself from a given number.

Example—What number is by 8 per cent. of itself more than 351? or 351 is 8 per cent. more than what number?

Example—My flock of sheep increased 8 per cent.; I then had 351. How many had I at first?

Example—I lost 8 per cent. of my sheep, and had 299 remaining. How many had I at first?

Analysis. { First, find the per cent. represented by the given number—100 per cent.—8 per cent.=92 per cent. Second, proceed as in 3d case—299 is $\frac{92}{100}$ of what number.

As a part of the general review, give an example in the fundamental case, and let the pupils derive the other three cases from it.

Commission and Brokerage and Profit and Loss are but applications of simple percentage. Each presents itself under all the four cases, but requires no special additional teaching, except in regard to the technical terms employed.

Interest.—Teach the definitions of the terms—the distinction of simple from compound interest—the legal rate of U. S. and of the State of New York.

Note.—In classes of an average character, *one* good method will be found to give better results than *two or more.* Whatever method be employed, the pupils should, from the first, be carefully guarded against considering and calling the multiplier a concrete number.

If the six per cent. method be employed, it should be carefully analyzed, and the pupil should not be allowed to sacrifice sense to conciseness by such statements as "the half of 7 months is 3 cents-and-a-half"—one sixth of 24 days is 3 mills, &c., &c." As a preliminary to applying this method, the class should have a thorough training on such questions as the following:—In 2 years, 3 months, and 20 days, at 6 per cent. per annum, *what decimal fraction of the principal* is equal to the interest? At 7 per cent.? at 5? at 8? at 7½? &c.

Give examples involving the various forms of the difference of dates—the application of the six per cent. method to a given or ascertained number of days. Example:—Interest of $340 from Jan. 5th to July 2d, at 6 p. c. Examples involving the method when the year is estimated to consist of 365 days, should also be given.

Give examples in Bank Discount, and explain its relations to Compound Interest.

Note.—(On the derived cases of simple interest.)—In teaching the four derived cases of simple interest, begin with an easy example in the fundamental case, and from that derive the others in their order, being particularly careful to teach that, being derived, they all require division; that, to find the *rate,* the given interest is to be divided by the interest at 1 *per cent.;* to find the *time,* by the interest for 1 *year;* to find the *principal,* by the interest of a *principal of* $1; and that, in the fifth case, the given *amount* is to be divided by the *amount of* $1.

Give examples in True Discount, distinguishing carefully its differences in principle, and therefore of method from Bank and Commercial discount.

Partial Payments and Compound Interest should be very briefly treated, and with very simple examples.

The form and nature of a promissory note, and the meaning of the several terms applicable to it, and the forms of bills and receipts are included in the work of this grade.

ENGLISH GRAMMAR.

1. *Analysis, parsing, and construction* should be continued in this grade, the class of sentences employed being of a more difficult character, but still carefully kept within the prescribed limits of "easy complex and compound sentences." By these are meant such as involve: 1. Complex sentences containing simple adjunct clauses, or brief clauses used as subjects, objects, or attributes,—those containing long and involved or intricate phrases being reserved for the next grade; 2. Compound sentences, formed by the union of simple clauses, or complex clauses, such as those above described. The analysis should be minute, so as to keep before the pupil's mind the relations upon which grammatical distinctions are based. The simplest phraseology should be used.

2. The exercises in construction should be made to correspond with the advanced character of the analysis; and the pupils in the "short compositions" required to be written, should, as far as possible, exemplify the instruction in the other portions of the subject. They should be required to analyze and parse the defective sentences which occur in these compositions, so as to discover the inaccuracies and to apply the necessary principles and rules for their correction.

3. The exercises for the special purpose of accustoming the pupils to care and criticism in the use of language, should be continued.

HISTORY.

The teacher is particularly referred to the General Suggestions on U. S. History in the preceding grade.

The special work of the Third Grade is comprised in the following:

SYLLABUS OF TOPICS.

The French and Indian War.—This should be taught in outline, the principal points being:—The gradual extension of the English and French settlements, leading to conflicting claims—the explorations and posts of the French in the valleys of the Mississippi, the St. Lawrence, and the Lakes—Marquette and La Salle—the debatable land on the upper Ohio—relatively small population of Canada—the building of Fort Du Quesne, 1754—Colonial Congress at Albany, 1754—Braddock's and Johnson's expeditions, and their results, 1755—Monckton's expedition,

1755—cruel expulsion of the Acadians—capture of Oswego, 1756—Fort William Henry, 1757—siege and capture of Louisburg, 1758—repulse at Ticonderoga, 1758—concentration of French forces at Quebec, by abandoning nearly all other posts—battle of Quebec, 1759, results—Treaty of Paris, 1763—its conditions.

In teaching the French and Indian War, let the ten dates marked be studied by the *years* only. Read, but do not memorize, the *details* of military movements and events—fix the sequence of events—use the map.

In the review, let the pupil tell very briefly of Washington, Braddock, Johnson, Monckton, Amherst, Abercrombie, Howe, Wolfe, Dieskau, and Montcalm.

The second portion of the special work of the grade, is:

The Outlines of the Revolutionary War.—(Teach as in the French and Indian War.)

Causes of the Revolution.—Navigation Acts.—Restriction of Colonial manufactures,—effects of war on the national debt of England—taxation without representation—the Stamp Act, 1765; its nature—causes which led to its repeal—the Tea Tax—riot in Boston, 1770,—the Boston "Tea Party," its immediate causes, and its consequences—nature of the Port Bill, 1774—first Congress at Philadelphia—its measures—*Lexington, April* 19, 1775—its effects upon the country—Bunker Hill—siege of Boston,—Washington appointed Commander-in-Chief—evacuation of Boston, and subsequent general drift of military events towards the west and south—*Declaration of Independence, July* 4, 1776,—battle of Long Island—its purposes and results—retreat to the Delaware—capture of the Hessians at Trenton—Princeton—La Fayette—British move on Philadelphia, 1777—Chad's Ford—its consequences—Burgoyne's invasion, its route and purpose, 1777—Schuyler—Burgoyne's disasters—Gates—the two battles of Stillwater—Clinton's movements—*Burgoyne's Surrender, October*, 1777—its far-reaching consequences—the French alliance and assistance—British retreat from Philadelphia—battle of Monmouth, 1778—New York the base of the British—destruction along the coasts of Connecticut and Virginia—Wyoming—battle of the Chemung, 1779—it breaks forever the power of the Iroquois—Paul Jones—Charleston captured, 1780—large numbers of Tories in the south—consequent years of guerilla warfare—Sumter—Marion—Gates at Camden—destruction of his army, and of Sumter's force—Arnold's treason—the mutiny at Morristown, 1781—its causes—condition of the army—Robert Morris—Arnold's ravages—Greene's retreat—battles in Carolina and their consequences—Cornwallis at Yorktown—combination of the French and American forces—*Surrender of Cornwallis, October*, 1781—its effects in America and England—Treaty of Paris, 1783—its terms—condition of the country.

Articles of Confederation, 1776–1777–1781—the government before 1781—after 1781—Shay's rebellion, 1786—leads to a convention to revise the Articles—a new *Constitution* devised instead, 1787—adopted by the States—*goes into operation*, 1789.

Natural Philosophy.

1. The direction to use "a simple text-book" is not to be interpreted as doing away with oral instruction in this branch. On the contrary, the proper use of the text-book is as an aux-

iliary, as a general guide to the teacher in the selection of subjects, and as an important help to the pupil in preparing at home for the recitation of a lesson which has been previously explained and illustrated in the class-room.

2. Any system of procedure which omits this preliminary oral instruction is certainly not worthy of the name of *teaching.* The text-book should be indeed brief and simple, and its illustrations necessarily few. But the teacher is to supply the further illustration and experiment which will certainly be found to be necessary; it is also of especial importance that the pupils should themselves be in every way encouraged and led to state such instances of these applications of the principles they have been taught, as *they* can themselves discover in the phenomena and incidents of their daily life, at home, in the street, the shop, and the school, so that, as far as possible, they may form habits of observation and reflection.

3. The teacher will find a wide difference in the readiness with which pupils will conceive and apply scientific principles. With a few, the bare statement of a principle will often enable them to point out its simpler applications. The results of a certain order of experiments, and the simpler deductions from them, will be promptly anticipated by such minds. But it will not be so with all; and with some, only by careful and repeated illustration will the principles which interpret the facts presented, be clearly apprehended. In all experiments the pupils themselves should be made as far as possible participants. In reviews they should be called upon to repeat the experiments or statements made by the teacher or given in the text, and to give the proper explanation. They should be encouraged to try further experiments for themselves at home, and then to furnish an account or a repetition of them in the class-room, if possible.

4. The teacher will also particularly remember that it is not necessary to follow slavishly the exact order or selection of topics given in the text-book. The teacher, and not the book, should be the master. An intelligent pupil will not be long in

finding out whether or not the statements in the text are the limit of his teacher's acquisitions. The great majority of young minds are hungry for this sort of knowledge, and it will unquestionably be the teacher's fault if that appetite is not at the same time both gratified and stimulated.

5. Great care should be taken, when the scientific meaning of a common term differs greatly from the popular one, to point out clearly such difference, in order that the pupil may not be misled by thinking that he knows that of which he is really ignorant. Among the many cases in which this will be found necessary, the terms *porosity*, *porous*, *solid*, and *impenetrability* may be taken as instances. It is by no means necessary that the pupil should be able to give an exact and comprehensive scientific *definition* of such terms; a few analytical questions by the teacher will readily show if the subject is understood.

6. When a lesson from the text-book is to be given for home study, it should first be carefully illustrated and explained. No teacher will be likely to do this as well as he should, if he give the subject no thought until about to assign the lesson. After receiving these explanations the pupil will be far less liable to misconceive or, as sometimes happens, to utterly fail to comprehend the statements of the text. As far as the subject will allow, he should be led through the medium of *experiment* to a knowledge of the *facts*. The facts once ascertained, the *principles* underlying them may be deduced. A limit will, sooner or later, be reached, where the more recondite parts of the subject, so far as they may be entered upon, *must be taught empirically*, in consequence of the pupil's limited knowledge of other departments of science.

For instance, suppose that the teacher has already experimentally established in his pupil's mind a general idea of the terms *force* and *gravity*, and that he now wishes to lead him to know that "the *weight* of a body is the *measure* of the *force* of *gravity*" acting upon it, and after that to establish the *law of its variation*. Let the teacher or one of the pupils borrow a common spring-scale—the smaller and simpler the better—let a pupil *pull*, and at the same time notice that he is exerting a *force*, that the position of the index will vary with the *degree* or *amount* of force, that the *motion* is in the *direction* of the force, however the instrument may be held; now place a succession of heavy bodies in the scale, and let him notice that the *effects* are identical with those produced by his muscular force. He will no longer *vaguely* conceive that the effect produced upon the scale is because the body is *heavy* (which was to him a vague term), but because the earth actually *pulls* it as he did, though no connecting bond is visible, as when *he* pulled. A knitting-needle suspended and balanced upon a thread and acted upon by a simple magnet, will clearly convince him that a *force* may be exerted by one body upon another without actual contact. You have clearly defined for him the idea that "the weight of a body is the measure of the earth's attraction upon it." If now you wish to teach the law of the *variation of the weight* of a body of invariable mass, as should indeed be done, the next step must be *empirical*. The pupil's deficiency in mathematics forbids any other course of procedure. The "Law of Gravitation" must be *stated to* him, together with the reason for so doing without proof. It will develop in many a mind an earnest desire to supply that deficiency. The law of the *variation* of weight may now be readily *deduced* by first adding to the pupil's mathematical knowledge the technical meaning of the term *square*, and then giving a variety of simple arithmetical problems to illustrate it.

7. There is, perhaps, no graver or more common error in relation to this subject, among earnest teachers who are called upon to teach it, than the notion that this requires expensive or complicated apparatus. The very contrary is indeed the case in the great majority of instances. Expensive apparatus, with its show of brass and glass, has a direct tendency to repress the most precious element and evidence of a teacher's success—experimenting at home by the pupils themselves. The principles of the *lever* may be just as well developed by means of a pen-handle, a pointer, or a window-pole, as by a polished brass or steel bar; a large spool makes an excellent *wheel and axle*, a ribbon-block a good single pulley, fixed or movable, a slate, a book, or a shingle, an *inclined plane;* a pocket-knife will

soon furnish a good *wedge* from a little piece of board, while the use of the blade itself is an excellent illustration of the application of the principle, and a large screw or a discarded auger-bit, with a knitting-needle or a pen-holder for a lever, makes an efficient *single screw*. And so through every department of the subject. Nothing marks more fully the ability of a teacher than fertility in such resources. Strings, tops, balls. and marbles; pop-guns, potato-mills, bean-shooters and putty-blowers, and the thousand and one nameless articles to be found in pupils' pockets, furnish an exhaustless mine of apparatus, and good apparatus too, for the skillful teacher. The immortal Dalton wrought out his atomic chemical theory with apparatus which may be excelled in many a junk or old bottle shop, and the teacher, determined to succeed, will find that "where there is a will there is a way."

SECOND GRADE.

Outline Course.

Reading.—Of the grade of a Fifth Reader, with spelling and definitions, as in the Third Grade.

Etymology.—With the analysis of words and their formation from given roots.

Mental and Written Arithmetic.—Through square root and its simple applications; problems as in the preceding grade.

Outlines of Physical Geography.

English Grammar.—Continued, with analysis, parsing, and construction, and the correction of false syntax; also composition. The exercises in analysis to be such only as are required to show the general structure of sentences.

History of the United States.—Outlines completed; events and dates as in the preceding grades.

Astronomy, elementary.—The solar system, with an explanation of the ordinary phenomena. A simple text-book to be used.

Natural Philosophy.—Simple outlines completed, to include Acoustics, Pyronomics, Optics, Magnetism, and Electricity.

DIRECTIONS, Etc.

Reading.

1. In this grade, the simple principles of elocution, taught in the preceding grades, should be carefully reviewed, and exercises to cultivate the voice, and confirm habits of distinct articulation should be continued to some extent. The *rationale* of good reading should, as occasion offers, be more fully explained, particularly as regards emphasis and modulation. Emotional reading should receive a fair share of attention. In the male schools, exercises in declamation and recitation will be appropriate as an auxiliary.

2. The pieces read, being of a higher order of style and subject, should receive a more careful analysis on the part of the teacher, so as, by interrogation, to lead the minds of the pupils to a proper understanding of their subject-matter, and enable them to obtain all the *information* and *culture of mind* which they may be made the vehicle of imparting. Much time is apt to be misspent in this grade by simply permitting the pupils to read mechanically and listlessly pieces of difficult prose and poetry, which by earnest teaching might be made to fix on the minds, and often in the hearts, of the pupils so much that is valuable. Few tests are so thorough of the earnestness and skill of a teacher as the teaching of reading in this and the next grade. The subject, the style, the difficult or unusual words, the allusions, the course of reasoning, mode of treatment, &c., may all be made the basis of useful investigation by the pupil or comment by the teacher.

3. The pieces read should comprehend a sufficient variety, both as to style and subject, to afford scope for what is above suggested. They should include didactic, narrative, argumentative, and oratorical selections; extracts from distinguished writers in history, biography, popular science, &c., as well as in the various departments of poetry; an important object of the instruction being to give a taste for reading more fully the works or compositions from which the extracts are made. Some account of the authors should be given in connection with the lessons.

ETYMOLOGY.

1. The *prefixes* and *suffixes* learned in the preceding grades should be reviewed by appropriate exercises involving the application of *easy roots*. For this purpose such words as the following may be used:—drunk*ard*, thrall*dom*, dep*th*, *ab*duct, vers*ion*, loc*al*,—involving English, or Anglo-Saxon, and Latin affixes only.

2. Next, the exercises should involve the use of easy *Latin* roots, such words as the following being used:—a*vert*, ad*vert*, con*vert*, per*vert*, &c.—*verse*, *vers*ion, di*verse*, &c. The application of various affixes, so as to form several words from the same root, will serve to impress the meaning of the root, *in its various forms*, on the mind of the pupil, as well as to review the affixes. *Latin words* need not be taught.

3. After a few exercises of this kind, words containing miscellaneous roots may be used, as pre*dict*, sub*mit*, re*ject*, in*vade*, &c.; then words containing prefixes and suffixes, as Sub*miss*ion ob*ject*ion, con*flu*ent, pro*ced*ure, &c.; care being taken at first to select such words as are *regularly* formed, and the literal signification of which exactly or nearly agrees with the actual meaning as used.

4. The following form of *analysis* is suggested:—*Abduct*—formed from the root *duct*, which means *to lead*, and the prefix *ab*, which means *away*. Hence, *abduct* means *to lead away*. Actual meaning, *to take away by stealth;* as, "They tried to *abduct* the child from his parents."

5. In this form of analysis, the *root* and its meaning are first stated; next, the *suffix;* then, the *prefix ;* and then the literal meaning of the word, to be followed in all cases by the actual meaning, which is to be exemplified in a sentence.

6. After the pupil is sufficiently initiated in the method so as to analyze words with some degree of facility, the principal *Latin roots* should be taken up and taught exhaustively, alpha-

betically, or in the order of their difficulty. These should be followed by a few of the *Greek roots,* suffixes and prefixes, to be followed by the French or other foreign roots. The Anglo-Saxon, or English, roots should, if taught at all, follow these. All beyond the Latin roots, and, if necessary, some of these, may be reserved for the First Grade.

7. Exercises in the "formation of words from given roots" should form a prominent part of the exercises used to familiarize the pupils with the meaning of the *roots,* as well as the meaning of words derived from them. For the purpose of this instruction, the English form of the root is all that needs to be taught, In this way the subject will be freed from much complexity. Thus, after analyzing the word *dentist,* the pupil gives, as far as he can recall to mind, the words derived from the root *dent;* as, *dent*al, *dent*ate, *dent*oid, *dent*ition, *dent*ifrice, *dent*iform, in*dent,* &c. Words such as *dentistry* are to be considered as of *secondary* formation, and to be analyzed by considering *dentist* the primitive. In this way the analysis of a very large class of words will be greatly simplified.

GEOGRAPHY.

Outlines of Physical Geography.

1. Some departments of physical geography, though perhaps not known by that name, have always been the necessary introductory element to the most rudimentary outline of political geography.—Describing the course of a river, the position of a peninsula or a cape, the direction of a mountain chain, or the boundaries of a continent, is as truly a part of physical geography, as is the explanation of the oscillation of the tropical rain-belt, of the formation and transport of icebergs, or of the theories of the trade-winds and ocean currents.

2. The physical geography specially prescribed in this grade is a comparative science. It considers the world as an organic whole, and presents the planetary conditions, the mutual re-

lations of all its parts, internal and external—the land, the sea, and the atmosphere,—the geographical distribution and conditions of the various forms of vegetable and animal life, and of the various races of mankind.

3. In the brief time that can be allowed to so comprehensive a subject in a single grade, it is obvious that only the simplest outline can be presented. The work has been carefully prepared for in the geography of the preceding grades, to which attention is here specially invited.

4. A synopsis of the points included in the grade is here appended. If a text-book is used, *the teacher should first be thoroughly familiar with its contents*, so that it may be employed principally as a reading or reference-book from which appropriate *selections* may be read in the class. If any other course be pursued, most of the text-books treat the subject so extensively that the pupil will necessarily leave it, as well as the grade, with only an unfinished foundation and no superstructure.

SYALLABUS OF TOPICS.

The Earth as a Globe,—its dimensions—probable condition of its interior (very brief)—its surface, as land, water, and atmospheric envelope. *The Earth as a Planet*—the zones and their causes—the land divided, the ocean not—comparative extent of each—land surface (omit geology), the continents—their direction, contour, elevations—the great mountain systems of the globe, volcanoes—theory of (brief)—distribution of volcanoes—the plateau belts—the great plains (use blackboard and rough chalk diagrams of sections)—the great islands and archipelagos, their distribution and arrangement.

The Ocean,—its subdivisions and great arms—its level—its great currents, their function, and some one theory of their origin (very brief).

The Atmosphere,—its constituents—vital importance of its watery vapor and its carbonic acid—evaporation from the ocean surface, and especially in the torrid zone.

The Winds,—The Trades, the Counter-trades—theory of (very brief) region of variable winds—(very brief) the winds as carriers of ocean vapor.

The Great Rain-belt,—its oscillations—tropical rainy and dry seasons—the mountains as condensers—illustrations.

Drainage,—the river systems of the several continents—their existence and direction in relation to the winds and mountain ranges—causes of deserts—illustration—lakes—snow on mountains and in frigid zones—glaciers, their origin and motion (very brief)—icebergs, their origin.

Vegetation (very brief),—warmth and moisture necessary to—general characteristics of tropical vegetation—well-known examples of subtropical and temperate regions—examples of arctic regions—examples of the great forest belts—prairie belts—desert belts—effects of various plants on human industries and development (very brief).

Animals (very brief),—characteristics of the several zones and continents—examples.

Man,—the various races, their proportion, leading peculiarities, and distribution.

The pictures and illustrative diagrams and maps of any good text-book will, if properly used, very greatly simplify and expedite the study of nearly every department of the subject, and will render definite ideas that might be otherwise vague.

ARITHMETIC.

1. In this grade, the teaching consists in large part of a review of what has gone before, with exercises sufficient in number and difficulty to familiarize the pupils with the principles, and render them expert and accurate in their application. For suggestions in regard to this part of the work, the teacher is referred to the preceding grades.

2. The advanced work comprises the following: *Exchange*, *Equation of Payments*, *Proportion*, *Partnership*, and *Square Root* with its simple applications. The exercises employed to teach these departments of arithmetic, should be of as practical a character as possible; and all the processes should be specially analyzed, the rules given being in all cases deduced from this analysis. A careful explanation of the *business transactions* involved in any of the rules or their applications, should always be given before the pupils are required to solve the problems. Failure more frequently arises from a want of this knowledge than from a deficiency in arithmetical attainment.

3. The following *syllabus* contains a brief summary of what is suggested to be taught in this grade.

SYLLABUS OF TOPICS.

1. EXCHANGE.—Its nature; bills of exchange; par of exchange; acceptance; domestic exchange—to include two cases:—1. To find the cost of a draft when its face and the rate are given; 2. To find the face, the cost and rate being given; foreign exchange, including the consideration of bills on England and France (cases as in domestic exchange); analysis as in percentage.

2. EQUATION OF PAYMENTS.—Cases: 1. To find average time of payment, when the items have the *same date*, but different credits; 2. When the items have different dates; 3. To find the average time for paying balance of account, having both debits and credits. *Analysis*, on the principle of *interest*, reducing each principal concerned to $1.

3. PROPORTION.—Ratio; proportion defined; relation of antecedents and consequents; ratio of 4 to 12, 4 : 12,$=\frac{4}{12}$, method of finding the missing term; simple and compound proportion distinguished; problems involving each (these problems should be only such as are required to illustrate the principle, since they are ordinarily to be solved by analysis previously given).

4. PARTNERSHIP.—Terms defined. Cases: 1. To find each partner's share when the profit or loss is divided according to capital only; 2. To find it when time is considered. *Analysis*, fractional, or by means of proportion.

5. SQUARE ROOT.—Involution and evolution defined; simple examples of each; powers of roots; illustration of what is meant by finding the square of a number; what is meant by square root. Illustrate by *simple powers*, integral and fractional,—common fractions and decimal fractions (the latter carefully). Problems in which the root contains denominations other than units. Illustrate by geometrical construction (square of the sum of two lines).

The following are specimens of "simple applications," which may be taught in this grade:—1. Given the *area*, to find the side of the square containing it.

2. Given the length and width of a rectangle, to find the side of a square equivalent to it.

NOTE.—In teaching the pupils how to find the area of a rectangle, avoid giving the erroneous impression that we absolutely multiply the length by the width as expressed by *denominate numbers*. Show that the number of *superficial units* corresponding to the *linear* units of the length, is multiplied by the number (abstract) of linear units in the width. Thus, if the length be 10 feet, and the width 5 feet, the area must be 5 times 10 square feet, equal to 50 square feet.

3. Given any two sides of a right-angled triangle, to find the other side. Teach and *illustrate* the geometrical theorem on which this problem depends. Give various questions requiring an application of this problem.

4. Every *topic* to be treated in this grade should be introduced by *mental exercises*, the slate being used only when the numbers involved are too large for intellectual calculation. The pupils should be constantly practiced in this mental work. The *text-book* in mental arithmetic should be sparingly used; and great care should be exercised in assigning lessons for home-study in this branch.

ENGLISH GRAMMAR.

1. In this grade, it is required that the pupils should be exercised in the *analysis* and *parsing* of sentences of a higher grade of difficulty. Those of anomalous or peculiar construction should be avoided. The analysis, except for review, should be only in outline, so as to show the general " structure," and enable the pupil to see clearly the relation of the clauses or members. This is essential to a correct and definite understanding of the *meaning* of the sentence, as well as for the application of rules having reference to the construction of sentences. Some knowledge of *punctuation* should be imparted in this connection.

2. The following sentence analyzed will illustrate the requirements, in this respect, of this grade:

" Pay the debts which thou owest; for he who gave thee credit relied upon thy honor, and to withhold from him his due is both mean and unjust."

Analysis.—This sentence consists of two members: 1. " Pay the debts," &c., to "owest;" 2. " He who gave thee," &c., to " unjust." These members are connected by "for."

The first member contains the clause "which thou owest," used as an adjunct of "debts."

The second member consists of the two clauses: "He who gave thee," &c., to " honor," and " To withhold," &c., to " unjust."

This should be followed by the *parsing* of the most important words, which will show whether a more minute analysis of the sentence should be required of the pupil or not.

3. As far as may be necessary, the *structure* of the sentence, discovered by analysis, should be made the subject of criticism, with reference to its *clearness* in expressing the meaning intended to be conveyed, its *propriety, unity, harmony,* &c. The thought itself may be, to some extent, analyzed, and subjected to critical remark.

4. The *parsing*, as an application of the rules and principles peculiar to our own language, should also, as far as possible, be so conducted as to have a *critical* end in view. This will greatly improve the pupils in their use of language, by rendering them more alert in discovering inaccuracies, as well as impressing more deeply upon their minds a knowledge of the rules by which they should be guided in expression.

5. *False Syntax—Composition.*—Exercises in the correction of *false syntax* should be abundantly used in this grade. The construction of sentences should assume the character of extended composition, the themes being selected by the pupils themselves or assigned by the teacher. Of course, care should be taken that the themes are of a simple character—appropriate to the mind of a child, and cultivated to awaken thought, not to repress it, as is too often the case when difficult subjects of an abstract or comprehensive character are chosen for the exercise.

HISTORY OF THE UNITED STATES.

For general suggestions see Fourth Grade.

Syllabus of Topics.

1789—1797—*Washington's Administration—Domestic History.*—Cabinet leading measures—States admitted—their former relations.

Note 1.—*Read* the Indian war. The teacher will give a brief statement concerning Boone, Clark, the original extent of Virginia, and the Ordinance of 1787. *Foreign* relations. Trouble with France and its cause.

Note 2.—Give, orally, a very brief outline account of the French Revolution, the resulting relations of France and England and of Europe generally ; the continuance of these wars to 1815. Refer particularly to the fact that political differences in the United States were, to a great extent, based upon our foreign policy, and that we were at last drawn into the vortex of the great European wars in 1812.

Refer also to Washington's Farewell Address, and give, briefly, a very few of its leading points.

1797—1801—*Adams' Administration.—Foreign* relations.—Continued troubles with France. *Domestic* history.—Unpopular measures—the death of Washington—removal of the Capital.

1801-1809—*Jefferson's Administration.—Domestic History.*—Admission of Ohio—its previous relations. The Louisiana purchase, its immediate and subsequent importance. Hamilton and Burr, 1804—a sketch of the history of each. Fulton's first steamboat, 1807. *Foreign* relations.—Tripolitan war, 1801-1805, its causes and results.

NOTE.—Read the detail, if given.

The state of Europe, and the importance of our carrying-trade. Extraordinary measures of France and England in relation to the rights of neutrals. English claims of right of search and impressment—bearing of the impressment claim upon our naturalized citizens, and our national honor. "Once a subject, always a subject." Affair of the Leopard and Chesapeake, 1807. Orders in Council and the Milan Decree, 1807. Embargo, 1807-1809. Non-intercourse Act, 1809.

1809-1817.—*Madison's Administration.* The entire interest centers in the *Foreign* relations—they control the *Domestic* history. Berlin Decree abolished, 1810.

NOTE.—*Read* the affair of the Little Belt—Indian War.

War declared June 19, 1812—its two chief causes.

NOTE.—*Read* the detail of the military and naval operations; show briefly in outline, first, the aggressive expeditions into Canada, from Detroit to the St. Lawrence; their general failure; second, the smallness of the navy—its brilliant success, but little direct influence on the fortunes of the war, excepting on the Lakes—utter destruction of American commerce; third, the aggressive expeditions of the British, the Americans being chiefly on the defensive after 1812. Indian war in the West and Southwest. Invasions from Canada. Blockade of all important ports. Naval and military expedition against Washington and Baltimore Invasion by the way of Lake Champlain. Expedition against New Orleans, and its purposes—final repulse of all these attempts, and similar fate of renewed aggressions of the Americans against Canada. Destruction of the Indian power.
Give the sequence of leading events, omitting the dates, except as to years.

The Hartford Convention—its alleged purposes—its effects. Treaty of Peace, December, 1814. A part of the general pacification of Europe upon the fall of Napoleon. The causes of the war not even alluded to in the treaty. Have these questions ever been settled? If so, when and how?

NOTE.—Read the second Barbary war, 1812-1815—its causes and results.

1817-1825—*Monroe's Administration.—Domestic* History—Missouri Compromise, 1820. Formation of new parties on questions of commerce and finance. Whigs and Democrats. The leading questions until 1845. *Foreign* relations.—Purchase of Florida. The Monroe Doctrine, 1822, its origin and importance.

1825-1829—*John Quincy Adams' Administration.*—Tariff of 1828—leads to the defeat of the Whigs and the election of Jackson.

1829-1837—*Jackson's Administration.—Domestic* History—United States Bank. Nullification, 1832. Clay's Compromise. *Foreign* relations.—French Indemnity.

1837-1841—*Van Buren's Administration.*—Panic of 1837. Sub-Treasury Bill, 1840. Political revolution.

1841-1845—*Harrison—Tyler's Administration.* — *Domestic* history. Bankrupt Law. Dorr's Rebellion. *Foreign* relations.—The Maine boundary. Annexation of Texas.

1845–1849—*Polk's Administration.*—*Domestic* relations now give direction to *Foreign* policy. Oregon boundary—its yet unsettled point in 1872. Chain of causes leading to the Mexican war. Boundary claimed by Texas. Mexican war, May, 1846, to Feb., 1848.

NOTE.—*Read* the details; give the leading military events in sequence, omitting all dates excepting years. Teach with the following grouping: Northern operations—Taylor east of the Rio Grande—west of it. Wool—Kearney—Doniphan—Fremont. Southern operations: Scott's campaign.

Treaty of Guadaloupe Hidalgo—its terms. Discovery of California gold in 1848—its important subsequent influence upon the national development.

1840–1853—*Taylor and Fillmore's Administration*—Slavery question the leading element in subsequent history. California question, 1850—its alleged relation to the Missouri Compromise. Death of Taylor. Clay's Compromise Bill, 1850.

1853–1857—*Pierce's Administration.* — Effects of the Fugitive Slave Bill. Kansas-Nebraska Bill, 1854—it violates the Missouri Compromise. Rise of a new party, "Free-soil" or Republican. Civil war in Kansas, its causes, flow of immigrants into the Territory.

1857–1861—*Buchanan's Administration.*—Kansas troubles. John Brown's affair—its effects. Split of the great Democratic party. Four Presidential candidates. Election of Lincoln. Extreme doctrine of State Rights. Secession of South Carolina, Dec., 1860. Fort Sumter. More States secede. Confederate government formed, Feb., 1861.

1861–1865—*Lincoln's Administration.*—Civil war. Fort Sumter, April 12, 1861. Effects upon the North. President's proclamation. More States secede, making eleven in all.

NOTE.—*Read* the details of the war; show the importance of foreign intervention, and the efforts on both sides in regard to it.

In the review show that the operations of the Confederates were mainly defensive, except in the great sorties of Lee at Antietam and Gettysburg, of Hood at Nashville, and of Early at Chambersburg—all of which were repelled. That the main objects of the aggressive movements of the Union troops were, 1st, the destruction of Lee's army; 2d, the opening of the Mississippi—that after the opening of that river by the fall of Forts Henry and Donelson, and the subsequent capture of New Orleans and Vicksburg, the lines were contracted by a movement from the north-west to the south-east, ending in Sherman's march from Atlanta to Savannah and Goldsboro'. The leading incidents will then readily fall into place.—Show the importance of the blockade, the chief function of the fleet—also, but very briefly, the enormous expenditure of men and money on both sides, and the measures by which they were obtained.

1865–1869—*Johnson's Administration.*—Death of Lincoln. The two subjects of leading importance—1st. Providing for the public debt; 2d. Reconstruction. The 13th Amendment. The President and Congress quarrel. Impeachment. The French in Mexico and demand of the United States Government. Purchase of Alaska. Laying of the Atlantic cable.

1869–1873—*Grant's Administration.*—Pacific Railway. 14th and 15th Amendments. Alabama question. Leading provisions of the Treaty of Washington. The Geneva Arbitration.

NOTE.—*Addenda.*—The rapid development of the country since 1815—the leading elements in that development. Emigration and Immigration. Erie Canal and Lakes as the great waterway. Steam and steam boats—Railways—Telegraphs. In the review include a notice of prominent men, such as Calhoun, Clay, Webster, Seward, Greeley, Fulton, Morse, &c., &c.

ELEMENTARY ASTRONOMY.

1. The teacher should, at first, endeavor to awaken an interest in the subject by referring to some of the most impressive and beautiful phenomena connected with the sun, the moon, the stars, planets, comets, and meteors. Endeavor to induce the pupils to observe more attentively these phenomena, and to excite their curiosity to know about them. Encourage them to ask questions in relation to what they observe; as, Why does the moon change its appearance? Why does the sun rise so far from the east, or set so far from the west at certain times in the year? What bright star was in the west on a certain night, at a particular time? and other such questions, some of which the pupils are, of course, to be told cannot be answered until they have further studied the subject. Then they will learn to study the science from nature as well as from the book.

2. Let the general phenomena of the heavens be first explained—the movements of the sun, moon, stars, and planets in relation to the horizon; the circles of daily motion—the difference between planets and fixed stars; how to distinguish some of the former, &c.

3. The following topics may then be taken up in their order: The *Earth*, its form, magnitude, motions, &c. *Circles* and *distances* on the Earth and in the heavens. *Day* and *Night*. The *Seasons*, &c. These topics should be illustrated by the use of a Tellurian, and *Problems for the Globe* should be used for the purpose of exercise and illustration.

4. Next, teach the general arrangement of the *Solar System*. Inferior and superior planets—their magnitudes, revolutions, position of orbits, periodic times, and apparent motions.

5. The *mathematical definitions* necessary for the proper understanding of this portion of the subject should be taught incidentally thereto.

NATURAL PHILOSOPHY.

For general suggestions, see Third Grade.

SYLLABUS OF TOPICS.

Acoustics—Preliminary. A general idea of the transmission of vibrations illustrated. The nature of sound. Sounding bodies. A medium necessary. The air as a medium. Other media. Limits of audibility of vibrations. Velocity in air and other media. Loudness does not alter the velocity. Reflection of sound. Echo, its causes and limits. Physical distinction of noise from music. Pitch in music. Influence of sound-boards. Tuning-forks, speaking-trumpets, speaking-tubes. Resonance—murmur of shell. The ear, its construction and action—the wonderful physical condition of the tympanum when listening to a full orchestra.

NOTE.—Many important experimental illustrations may be given by the aid of a simple tuning-fork.

Pyronomics—Heat—known only by its effects. Effect on the nerves—effect upon the constitution of bodies. Transmission of heat—three ways illustrated—air a bad conductor and worse radiator—important relation of this to clothing, to vegetation, &c. Heat as a sensation—relation of terms hot and cold. Sources of heat—quantity and effects of solar heat—its relations to physical geography. Source of the heat developed by friction—motion of mass converted into molecular motion. Heat only a mode of vibratory motion. Force as indestructible as matter. Source of heat in combustion. The thermometer—principles employed in its construction—nature of zero. Evaporation—its causes—effects on temperature of bodies. Phenomena of boiling—temperature of boiling water—why invariable at a given elevation—economic applications—why the boiling point varies with elevation—boiling in a closed vessel. The steam-engine—its essential elements and general principles—high-pressure and low-pressure engines.

Optics.—Light—moves in straight lines. Shadows. Sources of light. Vibratory nature of light (only refer to it). Velocity of light—how known. Law of intensity illustrated—Photometry by shadows. Non-luminous bodies—how seen. Reflection—its law—mirrors, and their uses (treat more fully of the plane mirror than of the others) Refraction—its simplest phenomena—its law. Lenses—uses of, especially the convex lens. Color—the prism and the solar spectrum—the order of the colors (refer very briefly to thermic and actinic rays). Phenomena of the rainbow—the colors of objects—primary colors. The eye and vision.

Magnetism.—Magnets, natural and artificial—forms of artificial magnets—polarity—attraction and repulsion—magnetic induction—temporary and permanent magnets—the Earth a magnet—magnetic needle.

Electricity.—Frictional electricity—conductors and non-conductors—electricity not a fluid, but a polarizing force, related to magnetism—attraction and repulsion—electric induction—insulators—effects of points—atmospheric electricity—its origin—lightning-rods—the flash—the white-hot air—the thunder. Popular fallacies—electric fluids—thunder-bolts—heat lightning—cause of thunder. Current electricity from chemical action—a battery, its wires and poles—polarized condition of the parts—how to develop heat and light—uses made of these—simple helix—simple galvanometer—magnetism developed by electric current—temporary magnet and magnetic telegraph.

FIRST GRADE.

OUTLINE COURSE.

Reading, Spelling, and Etymology—Continued.

Arithmetic—Mental and written, continued, with mensuration.

English Grammar—Continued, with composition, the latter to include impromptu exercises. Practice to be afforded in letter-writing, with instruction as to folding, directing, etc.

Astronomy—Outlines continued.

Algebra—Through simple equations.

General History—The outlines of Ancient and Modern.

Book-keeping.

Constitution of the United States.

The Rudiments of Plane Geometry—(First Book of Legendre, or an equivalent.)

Chemistry—Elementary principles and facts, without text-book.

DIRECTIONS, ETC.

READING, SPELLING, AND ETYMOLOGY—See previous grades.

ARITHMETIC.

In this grade, the pupils are to be carefully reviewed and practised in the principal rules comprised in the preceding grades. They are also to be taught the following:

1. *Cube Root*—How to extract it, with an illustration (by means of blocks) of the process. If the pupil has studied Algebra sufficiently, a demonstration by the Binomial Theorem may be given. The *formula* representing the cube of the sum of two quantities, will enable the pupil to remember clearly the details of the rule.

2. *Applications* of the Cube Root—to include the comparison of similar solids.

3. *Mensuration*, which should at least include the following cases:—1. To find the area of a parallelogram when the base and altitude are given; 2. To find the area of other quadrilaterals, with sufficient data; 3. To find the area of triangles;

4. To find the area of a circle; 5. To find the diameter and circumference of a circle when the area is given; 6. To find the solid contents, from sufficient data, of a cube, parallelopiped, prism, pyramid, cylinder, cone, and sphere; 7. To find the contents of a cask, or other vessel, with the requisite data.

English Grammar.

1. The exercises of this grade comprise those of analysis, parsing, and composition. Sentences of an irregular, or idiomatic construction, should be presented to the pupil, with the view to show how far their analysis can be made to harmonize with the usual syntactical rules, and to teach the just limits of their use. Anything bordering on *slang* should be discountenanced and condemned. An improper construction—that is, one that contravenes well-established rules and principles—should not be sanctioned by any ingenious analytical contrivance or substitution.

2. The exercises in analysis should embrace the careful and critical study of select passages from some of the best English and American writers; as Shakspeare, Milton, Pope, Cowper, Young, Bryant, Longfellow, &c., &c. Prose writers, such as Addison, Johnson, &c., should also be drawn upon for exercises,—always, however, with a critical end in view,—to discover and correct errors, as well as to find excellencies and beauties.

3. Such exercises, to however limited an extent it is possible to carry them, will always exert an important influence upon the pupils' style of composition, if not of daily speech. They will serve, moreover, to cultivate the taste of the pupils, and to awaken an interest in their minds in the study of English and American literature. A good reading-book will be found an important auxiliary in carrying on the instruction here suggested.

4. The exercises in composition should be, to some extent, *impromptu*, so as to develop that fluency and readiness in the written expression of thought which is of so much service in almost every sphere of life. The writing of letters, &c., as prescribed, should receive a very careful attention in this connection.

Astronomy.

1. The topics embraced in the preceding grade should be carefully reviewed in this grade, as far as may be necessary to secure thorough preparation for the advanced portions of the subject, which constitute the special work of the grade. The use of the globes should be continued, in order more fully to familiarize the pupils with the Doctrine of the Sphere, —so important to a clear understanding of astronomical facts.

2. The interest of the pupils in the observation of astronomical phenomena should be sustained by calling their attention as frequently as possible to facts which they can verify in this way. By degrees, the pupils should be induced to familiarize themselves with the locations, at different seasons of the year, at a given time by the clock, of the most conspicuous constellations and stars. The use of the Celestial Globe, or a planisphere, will furnish valuable aid in the accomplishment of this. The positions of the planets Jupiter, Saturn, Mars, Venus, and Mercury, among the stars, should be kept constantly in view, together with their apparent motions, and general progress eastward. The use of a good almanac will afford assistance in accomplishing what is here suggested; also in calling attention to the more unusual phenomena connected with eclipses.

3. The following topics should be especially treated in this grade:

Syllabus of Topics.

1. The Sun—its magnitude, real and apparent; distance from the earth (give a *general* idea of the manner of finding this, although a minute knowledge of *parallax* may be reserved for the more advanced part of the subject); solar spots—theory with regard to their cause, their apparent motions, what is deduced from this. The *Zodiacal light* may be briefly referred to in connection with the Sun.

2. The Primary Planets—in succession, commencing with Mercury, the pupil to learn the most important fact in relation to their orbits, magnitudes, telescopic appearance, synodic and sidereal periods, axial rotations, apparent motions, seasons, satellites, &c. The *Asteroids*, their orbits, &c. Any interesting facts in relation to the history of astronomical discovery should be communicated incidentally, as this will serve to make the subject more attractive.

3. The Moon—in a similar manner, teaching about its *phases* and their cause, its revolutions, periods, *Harvest Moon*, *Librations*, and a brief general description of the lunar surface (*Selenography*).

4. Eclipses—solar and lunar; total and partial, how caused; comparative frequency—ecliptic limits. *Transits*, their cause—why important.

5. Tides—flood and ebb, spring and neap, how caused; principal facts connected with them; the tidal wave; height of tide at different places—primitive and derivative tides.

6. Comets—their peculiar appearance, the different parts of which they are composed; different kinds of comets; periodic times of the comets of short period —interesting facts in relation to the *orbits, size, mass, density*, and apparent magnitude of conspicuous comets.

7. A brief account of *Meteors*, their supposed nature and origin—cause of the periodic displays of meteors.

8. Stars—classification—the constellations—names, classification of, brightest stars in each—apparent change in position due to *precession*; cause of precession; exercises in finding the constellations visible at any time; the *galaxy*; proper motion of the stars; multiple stars; variable and temporary stars; distances of the stars, how found; *parallax*, diurnal and annual.

9. Nebulæ—classification of; their nature and appearance; general location and appearance; the location and appearance of some of the most noted.

10. Time—how measured; solar, sidereal, and civil day; why the solar exceeds the sidereal day; why the solar days are unequal; equation of time; tropical, sidereal, and civil years, how and why they differ in length.

11. Astronomical Refraction—its effect upon the apparent positions of the heavenly bodies; variation at different altitudes.

12. General Review.

4. In giving instruction in this subject, its special office as a means of training the *conceptive faculty*, should be kept steadily in view. Facts of observation and facts of *inference* should be carefully distinguished. Apparatus and diagrams will afford some aid in enabling the mind to grasp the more difficult facts of inference; but the actual *observation* of the phenomena to be illustrated should precede, as far as possible, the use of these. Thus, a good *tellurian* will illustrate clearly the causes of the change of the seasons, and a diagram may be made to show the reason of their unequal duration; but the facts of these changes and inequalities must first be clearly apprehended by the mind. If this is done, the natural curiosity to know the cause will make the pupils more attentive to the instruction given. Cumbrous and complicated machinery, without the attentive observation of the natural phenomena, and the conceptions based upon them, rather serve to give false

notions than to impart clear ideas of the actual facts. A good *planisphere* will prove a valuable aid in the study of *uranography*.

5. Nor should the teacher fail, in connection with this instruction, incidentally to impress upon the pupils' minds that, in studying the laws and facts of the universe, he is contemplating the works of a beneficent Creator, infinite in wisdom and power. No subject is so well qualified as astronomy to give just ideas in this respect, and, while performing a peculiar and most important office in the training and development of the intellectual powers, to exalt the understanding, and give elevation and tone to the whole character.

ALGEBRA.

1. This subject is to be taught as a peculiar *mathematical language*, by means of which the relations of quantities and the result of their combinations may be expressed, and reasoning in regard to them may be facilitated. The symbols, both of *quantities* and *relations*, or *operation*, should at first be carefully taught and illustrated.

2. The *simple operations* of addition, subtraction, multiplication, and division, should not be exhaustively treated, as is usually done, before the pupil is made acquainted with the nature and use of equations. The *equation* is to Algebra what the *proposition* is to ordinary language. It is the means of definitely expressing a mathematical truth, either particular or general. *Inequations* (technically so called) express truths, but not exactly; as, when we say $x+y > 75$, we do not indicate *how much* the sum of x and y exceeds 5; but if we say $x + y = 6$, we express a precise fact. It is suggested, therefore, that *equations* be presented very soon after the preliminary explanation of the symbols employed. The examples of equations first presented should be of the simplest character; and their use in the solution of problems should be *objectively* shown. This can be done by employing a few very easy questions, such as are given in some of the text-books for mental solution; as, *What number is that, to the half of which, if* 5 *be added, the*

sum will be 11? The dullest pupil can be easily made to perceive the use of expressing that condition so that it can be clearly kept in view; as (x representing the unknown number), $\frac{x}{2} + 5 = 11$.

In solving such a problem, the successive steps or *processes of reasoning* should be kept in view. Thus, subtracting 5 from each number, the result (expressed by a second equation) is $\frac{x}{2} = 6$; and, multiplying by 2, the result (expressed by a third equation) is $x = 12$, which gives the solution. (Applied axiom to be referred to.)

Such an exercise, properly performed, will develop more intelligence than whole months of mechanically working out, by blind rules, long sums in addition, subtraction, multiplication, and division, such as Multiply $x^2 - 3x + 5$ by $x^3 - x^2 + 2$; Divide $x^3 - y^3$ by $x - y$, &c., &c. These exercises are proper in their place, but of themselves they have but little, if any, educational or practical value.

Syllabus of Topics.

1. Preliminary explanation of symbols, both *letters*, as representatives of quantity, and the signs of relation or operation, as, $+ \ - \ \times \ \div \ =$ &c.; exercises to familiarize the pupil with their significance and the mode of reading them,

Note.—It will be of great service to accustom the pupil to read algebraic expressions in such a way as at once to indicate their meaning; as, $a + b$, the sum of a and b; $a - b$, the difference between a and b; $a \times b$, the product of a and b, &c. Exercises in finding the numerical value of expressions, when particular values are attributed to the representative letters, will greatly aid in accomplishing this result. Thus, find the value of $\frac{a^2b - b^3}{c}$ when $a = 3$, $b = 2$, $c = 1$, &c.

2. Easy problems in arithmetic, the solution of which may be facilitated by the use of equations, the latter to be of the simplest form, and involving only an application of the pupils' acquired knowledge of symbols. This will at once show the pupils the value of the algebraic notation, and interest them in the study of the subject, as being of practical value.

3. *Mental practice* in solving such problems, by means of equations. Most of the text-books in use will afford a sufficient variety.

4. Practice in solving equations of this character; each equation to be read previously in the form of a problem; as $\frac{x}{3} - \frac{x}{8} = 10$, which may be read: What number is that, one-third of which exceeds one-eighth of it by 10?

The method of *clearing equations of fractions* and *transpositions* should be taught, not by applying mechanical rules, but as processes of analytical reasoning. Thus, in the equation above given, the pupil will easily be made to perceive, that the multiplication of both members by 24 will produce an equation without fractions. (The intermediate step $\frac{24x}{3} - \frac{24x}{8} = 240$ should be at first used.)

5. After the pupils have acquired a clear idea of the nature and use of equations, and some expertness in operating with those of a simple character, those of a more difficult or complex form should be presented,—giving occasion for the use of the operations of addition, subtraction, multiplication and division which can then be more exhaustively treated, with sufficient practice on the part of the pupil.

6. The nature of literal equations or *general expressions* should be then taught, and examples given, some of which may be made to involve an application of all these processes.

Such as the following are suggested:

(1.) $\frac{x + a}{b} - \frac{x - a}{c} = d$

(2.) $\frac{x - a}{b} + \frac{x - b}{a} = 2$

(3.) $\frac{x - a^2}{b} - \frac{x - b^2}{a} = 0$

(4.) $\frac{x}{a - b} - \frac{x}{a + b} = 1$

(5.) $\frac{(a + b)x}{a - b} - \frac{(a - b)x}{a + b} = \frac{1}{4}$

Such equations as the above involve much useful practice, not only in adding, subtracting, multiplying, and dividing, but also in fractions and in factoring. The latter should receive careful attention.

6. The method of solving equations containing more than one unknown quantity—involving the various methods of *elimination*—should follow this, and sufficient practice in the *solution of problems* should also be afforded. The latter, with the preparation herein indicated, may be made a most important aid in training the mind to careful and exact analysis, and logical reasoning—perhaps the most important object, generally, of the study, of this subject.

NOTE.—This syllabus is not designed to be entirely exhaustive, but to afford hints as to the order and method of presenting the most important topics.

GENERAL HISTORY.

1. The *General Suggestions* given in relation to United States History (see Grade Fourth), are, to a very great extent, applicable to this grade. The much greater extent of time to be covered in teaching ancient and modern history, together with the vast number and diversity of nations which it embraces,

necessitates, in a much greater degree, the fixing of a good outline in the mind of the pupil, as preliminary to a more minute study of the subject.

2. This outline should be brief, but should show clearly the chronological and geographical relations of the nations, the history of which is to be studied, and, to some extent, their ethnological relations. When this has been done, it will be perfectly easy to take up the history of any nation comprehended in this outline, and treat it intelligibly. The use of maps, charts, and synchronous tables, will aid very much in impressing firmly upon the pupils' minds such an outline as is here suggested. The maps used should show clearly and accurately the territorial extent and relations of the various nations generally treated of in ancient, mediæval, and modern history. All names of places referred to should be carefully pointed out on the map, so that their exact location may be constantly kept in view. This will aid the memory very much, as it brings into play the faculty of conception.

3. The *order of time* should be carefully kept in view at first, and the date (year) of each important event kept before the mind of the pupil. A few leading dates should be carefully memorized. After the history of different nations has been studied, the leading events of each should be arranged in synchronous tables. The reigns of contemporaneous sovereigns, for example, should be compared, and the connection of events in each carefully studied.

4. *Reviews*, such as are suggested in the United States History, by a chronological, geographical, and biographical arrangement of topics, should be given with sufficient frequency.

5. The following syllabus presents the topics which should be embraced in the outline above suggested:

SYLLABUS.

1. The nations and countries of the most remote antiquity—*Egypt* and *Ethiopia*, *Babylonia* and *Assyria*, *Lydia*, *Media*, *Syria* and *Palestine*, *Persia*. Of these only a brief sketch need be learned.

2. GREECE.—The mythologic period (very brief); the period from the beginning of the Persian war to the Roman conquest of Greece. This will include the rise and fall of the Macedonian Empire, with its divisions under Alexander's successors.

3. ROME.—The legendary period; the foundation of the Republic in its various stages, including the contests between the orders of Patricians and Plebeians; the successive wars with the Samnites, Carthaginians, &c.; the civil wars, including the triumvirates; the fall of the Republic, and the foundation of the Empire under Augustus. The territorial conquests should be shown in connection with this.

4. THE ROMAN EMPIRE.—Its territorial acquisitions and changes from Augustus to the division of the Empire at the death of Theodosius, including a brief sketch of the principal reigning emperors, and the invasions by the Goths, Huns and Vandals.

5. THE WESTERN EMPIRE—from Honorius to its fall under Augustulus (brief), including the barbaric invasions.

6. THE EASTERN EMPIRE—from Arcadius to the taking of Constantinople by the Ottomans; a brief sketch, including the wars with the Goths, Saracens, Seljuks, Mongols and Ottomans.

7. THE SARACENIC EMPIRE—a brief sketch of its foundation, its territorial conquests and extent, its divisions and its fall.

8. FRANCE—the invasion of Gaul by the Franks, and foundation of the *Merovingian Dynasty;* a brief sketch of it; the *Carlovingian Dynasty,* including Charlemagne's conquests, and the revival of the Western Empire; the *Capetian Dynasty,* to the end of the Reign of Louis XI. This will include the *Crusades.*

9. ENGLAND—a brief sketch of British History before the time of Egbert; from Egbert to the Tudors. (England may be studied first, if it is preferred.)

10. Other nations contemporaneous with England and France (very briefly).

11. MODERN HISTORY—in a similar manner; *England* and *France,* as the leading nations; other nations, including *Germany, Prussia, Russia,* &c.

12. AMERICAN HISTORY—not immediately connected with U. S. History.

Other parts of the world, as *China, India,* &c., may be omitted in this preliminary outline—which is all that is intended to be prescribed for the Grammar Schools.

6. This history should be so studied as to induce the pupils to read standard writers upon the most important topics. The instruction should embrace advice and direction as to the best writers in each period and nation. *Historical selections* will be found valuable for this purpose.

BOOK-KEEPING.

1. After the forms required in single-entry book-keeping have been taught, which should be quite brief, the nature of double-entry book-keeping should be explained, by showing the relation of *debit* and *credit*, and how the former in one account may be exactly balanced in another, so that one set of entries may be made to verify the accuracy of another, and thus prevent the admission of any errors which may not be readily discovered and rectified.

2. The *classification* of accounts should be followed by an explanation of the three books—Day-Book, Journal, and Ledger. Journalizing simple entries in the Day-Book should then be taught; and sufficient exercises given to impart readiness and accuracy in the process. The keeping of a simple and brief set of accounts will then render the whole process and theory intelligible to the pupils' minds, and will also render them sufficiently expert in their application.

3. All the common *business forms* should be taught; as the form of bills, receipts, bank checks, promissory notes, bills of exchange, invoices, &c., &c. *Business correspondence* should also receive some attention. It is of great importance to render the pupils expert in writing a good business letter. In every exercise fluency, legibility, and grace in penmanship should be carefully attended to. *Quantity* and *quality* should both be insisted on in this respect.

CONSTITUTION OF THE UNITED STATES.

1. The requirement to teach the *Constitution of the United States* applies to pupils of both sexes in this grade. It has been deemed essential that those who pass through the course prescribed for the Grammar Schools should have some knowledge of the simple principles and requirements of the organic law of the nation,—the distribution of the powers of the general government, and the rights, duties, and obligations of an American citizen.

2. The Constitution itself should be the text studied, the pupils being made familiar, as far as possible, with the language of the instrument, and also instructed in the meaning and intention of the several provisions. Several matters, purely technical, will need to be carefully elucidated; as *ex-post-facto laws, bills of attainder, habeas corpus*, &c., &c. The history, English and American, particularly the former, which is connected with these, will prove a most instructive and interesting subject for comment by the teacher.

3. Questions as to the construction of certain points in the Constitution, which have been in agitation during the past history of the Country, would prove, in the boys' classes especially, as far as time and opportunity may admit, useful for discussion, as tending to impart readiness in speech, as well as self-reliance and freedom in thought and opinion.

GEOMETRY.

1. This subject, from its extremely *abstract* character, is quite difficult for young students fully to comprehend. It is essential that the abstract ideas with which it is concerned should be developed in the minds of the pupils at the preliminary stage of the study; since, unless this is done, they cannot be profited by the instruction, nor, indeed, take any interest in it. They will, moreover, be wholly incapable of carrying on the processes of reasoning involved in the demonstrations, unless they clearly apprehend the nature of the truth to be proved, as well as of those assumed as premises, or arguments.

2. The first idea to be developed is that of a *solid*, as conceived in geometry, involving *three dimensions* of extension; next, that of a *surface*, abstracted from the solid, involving *two dimensions;* next, that of a *line*, abstracted from the surface, involving *one dimension;* and, lastly, that of a *point*, as indicative of a position in the line, or at either of its extremities, and involving *no dimensions*. These terms, reversing the order, should then be defined; namely, *point, line, surface, solid*. Unless these

fundamental conceptions are clearly and thoroughly impressed, upon the minds of the pupils, no true progress can be made.

3. The *classification* of lines and surfaces may then be taught, the fundamental idea used being that of *direction;* as of a straight line, *never changing* its direction; a curved line, changing it *at every point;* of a broken line, changing it at certain points. The classification of surfaces into *plane, curved* and *broken* may be made in an analogous manner.

4. With this, the idea of *parallel lines* may be made to harmonize by conceiving them as lying *side by side* (literal meaning of *parallel*), and all in the same direction, *i. e.*, tending to a point *at an infinite distance*, or tending to points at a finite distance, which, wherever assumed, are at the same distance from each other (the latter may be the easier to develop at first).

5. The idea of a plane *angle* should be made to harmonize with these conceptions of a straight line and parallel lines, being conceived as expressing the *difference* in *direction* of two straight lines that meet at a point.

NOTE.—This, it will be seen, harmonizes with the idea of parallel lines, which tend to a point at an infinite distance, and hence *never meet*, and cannot form an angle; while the straight lines that form an angle tend to a point at a *finite distance*, and meeting at that point, form the angle.

6. The definitions of Geometry form the groundwork of the subject, constituting the basis upon which all the subsequent reasoning rests; hence, it is very important that these definitions should be clearly understood and carefully committed to memory.

7. It is desirable, before the pupils are required to study demonstrations, that the different methods of *reasoning* should be carefully explained, and that they should, to some extent, be exercised in the same. This can easily be done by bearing in mind that geometrical truths have reference to a comparison of magnitude, and hence involve the idea of *equality* as a definite fact, and *inequality* indefinitely. Thus, it is required to be proved that the sum of the three angles of a triangle is *equal* to two right angles; also, that, of any two sides of a triangle, that which lies opposite to the greater angle is

the greater (not *how much* greater). Hence, as a preliminary exercise, the following might be given:—*Question*—If A is equal to B, and B is equal to C, how does A compare with C? *Answer*—They are equal. *Question*—Why is A equal to C? *Answer*—Because they are both equal to B. *Question*—How does that prove it? *Answer*—Because things that are equal to the same thing are equal to each other. *Question*—Can that be proved? *Answer*—It cannot; it is self-evident. *Question*—What are self-evident truths called? *Answer*—They are called *axioms*.

A variety of such exercises may be employed; and, in this way, the pupil, before beginning any formal demonstrations, may be made clearly to apprehend the nature of geometrical reasoning—so different from that which he has generally employed during all his previous studies, or which he uses in daily life. If the foundation here suggested is well laid, the pupil will soon find it as easy a task to *read* his geometry, and to learn it by *reading* (not *rote study*), as to read any other book of science.

8. Of course, in hearing recitations in geometry, the teacher should vary the method, so as to preclude entirely the possibility of any rote study, or merely *verbal recitation*. For this purpose, the *figures* employed should be different from those in the text-book, the *letters* used in connection with the figures should be changed, or numerals used in their stead. The demonstrations should sometimes be given without using either letters or numerals; and, in the case of such as are very easy, the figures themselves may be dispensed with. In most cases, the pupil should be required briefly to recapitulate the arguments employed.

9. The amount of ground to be covered in this grade is defined as the "First Book of Legendre, or an equivalent." The following Syllabus (intended only to be suggestive) embraces everything required.

SYLLABUS OF TOPICS.

1. Elementary definitions—axioms—symbols.

2. Theorems relating to straight lines, angles, and polygons: 1. *The sum of any two adjacent angles is equal to two right angles.* 2. *Vertical angles are equal to each*

other. 3. The various theorems pertaining to the angles formed by the intersection of two parallel lines and a third line. 4. Angles having their sides parallel are equal. 5. Triangles are equal, (*a*) when they have two sides and the included angle in each respectively equal; (*b*) when they have two angles and the interjacent side in each respectively equal; (*c*) when they have three sides in each respectively equal. 6. The sum of the three angles of a triangle is equal to two right angles. 7. The sum of the interior angles of a polygon is equal to twice as many right angles as the figure has sides, less four right angles. 8. The sum of the exterior angles of a polygon is equal to four right angles. 9. Theorems relating to a comparison of the perpendicular and oblique line drawn from the same point to the same straight line. 10. Only one perpendicular can be drawn from a given point to a given straight line. 11. The greater side of any triangle is opposite to the greater angle; and the converse. 12. The opposite sides and angles of a parallelogram are equal; and the converse. 13. Any problem, either after, or in connection with, these theorems, which can readily be performed; as, to construct an equilateral triangle, to bisect a given straight line, or a given angle, &c. In order to aid in the solution of these, it will be necessary to teach the definition of a circle, its construction, and parts.

Compass and ruler exercises may also be profitably interspersed.

CHEMISTRY.

1. The *general suggestions* in regard to oral instruction (see Eighth Grade) should here be carefully kept in view. The instruction required to be given in chemistry in this grade can only be very rudimental; but, as far as it extends, it should be *practical.* The chemistry of common things, or of every-day life, is what is designed to be taught.

5. Without apparatus, this instruction cannot, of course, be given objectively; but very much may be *conceptive.* A considerable portion, however, must consist in imparting direct information. The following syllabus is suggested:

Syllabus of Topics.

1. Elements—Chemical attraction—Atomic Theory—Nomenclature (brief).

2. *Important elements* described; as, Oxygen, Nitrogen, Carbon, Hydrogen: their principal compounds. The metals, oxides, salts.

3. The Atmosphere—its constituents—its relations to plants and animals.

4. The Earth—Relation of plants and animals to it. Soils—their constituents—Common Salt, Soda, Potash, Lime, &c.

5. Plants—what we obtain from them—Starch, Gum, Sugar, Lignin, Vegetable Oils, Albumen, Gluten, &c.

6. Animals—their food—Albumen, Fibrin, Casein, &c. How distributed in different kinds of food; digestion of food; respiration of animals—chemical changes affected by it.

7. Decomposition of plants and animals.

8. *Special topics*—Bread-making; glass-making; soap-making; fermentation; distillation; alcohol, &c., &c., &c.

SUBJECTS FOR EACH GRADE OF THE COURSE.

Penmanship.

Penmanship is prescribed to be taught in each grade of the Grammar School Course, in addition to the constant practice which is required in *slate-writing*. By means of the latter, if a due attention is given to it, much can be accomplished in insuring to the pupil readiness and fluency in the exercise of this art; but if he be allowed to fall into careless habits, his style of writing, both with pen and pencil, will be almost incurably vitiated.

The exercises in spelling from dictation, composition, &c., should be performed with punctilious accuracy, even if some sacrifice of rapidity be at first required. Of course, there should be a constant effort to improve both in rapidity and accuracy—*quantity* as well as *quality* being made a criterion of merit and success.

The slate-writing should, as far as it is practicable, exemplify the principles and methods formally taught in the lessons in penmanship. Pupils should not be permitted to violate in the one class of exercises the rules and precepts taught and practised in the other. This is especially applicable to the holding of the *pencil*, which should be sufficiently long to be held as a *pen*.

The lessons on *penmanship* should be methodical and progressive, whatever system may be employed. In the lower grades the exercises should be rudimentary, but the pupil should not be retained in them too long. He should be permitted to *write* as much as possible; making *strokes* and *curves* is not writing, although it may be valuable as leading to it. A few of such exercises will suffice.

Neither should the use of *trial papers* be carried to the extreme of withholding the pupil for a considerable time from the use of his copy-book, so that months are required to finish the latter. The pupil should be taught the necessity of doing everything as well as he can do it; but perfection in details should not be expected in the rudimental stages. It should, *from the first*, be deemed essential (at least *meritorious*) to execute the work prescribed with dispatch, provided there is no want of care or attention. *Festina lente*, however, is a motto that applies to the acquisition of this art, as well as others, in its first stages.

A proper distinction should be made between the lessons given to show the pupils how to write and the exercises designed to practise them on what they have thus learned. In the former, the whole class should invariably be occupied in the same work, the teacher explaining, and illustrating from the blackboard, the principles and methods which form the subject of the lesson; in the latter, practice being the object in view, it is not so essential that all the pupils should be doing the same thing at the same time, although even here it is a convenience to the teacher, since it facilitates supervision.

It should be carefully kept in view that the *hand* and the *eye* as well as the *mind* of the pupil are to be trained in this branch of instruction,—the *hand* to execute, the *eye* to discern, the *mind* to judge. These are not to be educated separately and successively, but simultaneously. The pupil must be taught to know what is the correct form of every letter, and his hand must be so trained by correct practice, that it will execute the dictates of mind and eye.

Hence a correct method of holding the pen, a proper position of the body while sitting at the writing-desk, and a suitable placing of the book or paper, are all indispensable pre-requisites to the acquisition of a good hand-writing. The first of these demands especial attention; and every lesson should, for some time, be introduced by distinct directions as to the proper method of holding the pen, and these the pupils should not be permitted to violate. With regard to the latter—position of body and position of book—a few simple directions will be all that are requisite.

The teacher should especially see that the pupils sit in such a position as to allow perfect freedom of motion of the right hand and arm, ease of respiration, and as much physical ease otherwise as the seat and desk will permit. The book should if possible, be provided with covers and blotters; the pens should be carefully cleaned at the end of each lesson, and changed as often as necessary, and the ink in the best condition. Each page of the book should end with the name of the pupil and the date.

In the higher grades,—the *first* at least—the writing of copies consisting each of a single line, should be discontinued; and paragraphs, verses, business forms, notes, superscriptions, &c., should take their place. The exercises in book-keeping should be made subservient to the instruction in penmanship —writing up the usual blank-books being made, to some extent at least, a substitute for the use of copy-books. Various styles of writing should be taught, as far as time and opportunity may permit,—as the business style, epistolary style, engrossing style, &c. This has reference to the Female as well as the Male Grammar Schools.

DRAWING.

Drawing is prescribed to be taught in each grade in the Grammar School course; and in addition to the ordinary lessons, "exercises in perspective and the delineation of objects" are required in the First, Second, and Third grades of that course (By-Laws, § 81).

The instruction should be carefully graded in every part of the course, and the progress of the pupils should correspond with that in other branches, as promotion is made from grade to grade. The following syllabus is suggested for the Grammar Schools:

SYLLABUS.

EIGHTH GRADE.—Review of the work prescribed for the Primary Schools,—straight lines, drawn in various positions and combinations, and divided into equal parts; rectilinear figures, as squares, triangles, rhomboids, &c.; also simple lessons in drawing from copies and objects.

SEVENTH GRADE.—Review of the Eighth Grade, as far as may be necessary, and drawing curved lines, and figures formed from them, as the circle, ellipse., &c.

Sixth Grade.—Review of the work of the preceding grades, to which add scrolls and simple geometrical solids in outline; as, the cube and parallelopiped. Show how to represent the latter in various positions.

Fifth Grade.—Review as far as may be necessary, and add other geometrical solids, in outline, as, cylinder, cone, pyramid, and prism; also, the outline of utensils and other objects in familiar use, which differ but slightly from these regular forms. Other simple objects may be copied from cards.

Fourth Grade.—Continued practice in the work prescribed for the preceding grades, to which add the sphere, oblate and oblong spheroids, and the hemisphere, with first lessons in shading, to show how the convexity of these various figures should be represented. The shading lines should be distinct, so that the proper mode of drawing them, as to direction and proximity, may be discerned by the pupils.

Third Grade.—Drawing on paper commenced, the work of the preceding grades to be reviewed briefly, as far as may be necessary. Special attention to be given to the drawing of rectangular solids from blocks in various positions, with a few simple directions as to perspective.

Second Grade.—Drawing on paper—Objects of regular form, in perspective, block combinations, &c., with shading. Copying, from cards, familiar objects; as parts of the human body, outlines of animals, &c.

First Grade.—Drawing from objects continued, with exercises in perspective. Crayon drawing. Copying pictures of animals, trees, and other objects, with easy landscapes, as far as the time may permit. In the Male Grammar Schools, simple lessons in architectural drawing may be given, as a substitute for a part of what is here suggested, when it is deemed proper or requisite.

When special teachers are employed, they should have the instruction especially of the 1st, 2d and 3d grades, but should, as far as practicable, supervise and direct the elementary work, so as to insure uniformity and harmony in the entire work of the school.

Vocal Music.

This branch of instruction includes "musical notation," with singing exercises, in both the Primary and Grammar Schools. In the former, where a special teacher is employed, the pupils, on completing the first grade, and before promotion to the Grammar Schools, should, at least, have been taught the following:

The staff, clefs, notes, rests, sharps, flats, naturals, and the other ordinary musical characters; also numerals and letters on the staff, with G clef; and they should be able to read by *letter* the notes without singing them. They should also be able to sing the intervals of the major scale with numerals from 1 to 8 inclusive, both ascending and descending the scale; also by skips of 1, 3, 5, 8, and 2, 4, 6, 8, &c., upward and downward. Beating time should be practised in the varieties of double measure. Easy melodic forms (with notes of equal length, at least) should also be read and sung, with a proper attention to a correct intonation, all shouting or forcing of the voice being carefully avoided. Simple melodies with words should be practised for the ordinary purposes of school singing.

The instruction here required should be given from the blackboard, or charts, in the objective method, as far as it is applicable, and with the constant view to prepare the pupils for the more advanced stages of musical instruction in the Grammar Departments.

In the *Grammar Departments for Boys* the following, at least, should be accomplished:

A review of the work of the Primary Department, and in addition thereto, an extension of the major scale beyond the octave upward to the third above the key note, and downward to the fourth below, the key note being pitched upon C on the first added line below the staff in the treble clef; also a knowledge of the letters in the F or bass clef, and the intervals in both clefs, with singing exercises in each. Pupils in these schools should be taught to sing in two parts, in the key of C, moving in *thirds* or *sixths;* also to transpose the first four major and minor keys beyond C major and A minor, writing the exercises on the slate both with numerals and letters. They should, also, be able to give the relative length of all the notes and rests, and to beat the time, and sing the exercises and tunes in one or in two parts. A class-book should be used in the Grammar Schools; and every lesson by the special teacher should comprehend instruction in musical notation. No pupil in these schools should be permitted to sing whose voice is undergoing change.

In the *Female Grammar Schools*, the above should be taught with the following additions: All the letters in both clefs, from C C, in the bass to C in alt, in the G clef; transposition in all the keys in the major and minor scales, with singing exercises in each, both with numerals and letters. The pupils should be able to write the perfect chords of all the major and minor scales, and determine all the keys by the signature. Modulation should also be taught, and practice given in singing studies in all the keys, in *syncopation*, in *legato*, in *staccato*, and in *triplets*. The pupils should be able, after completing the course, to read in *plain song* in two parts, written in whole, half, and quarter notes, and in double, triple, quadruple, or sextuple movement.

COURSE OF INSTRUCTION

IN THE

GERMAN LANGUAGE.

---

§ 87. (By-Laws of the Board). The following shall be the course of instruction in the German language, to be pursued in connection with the several grades of the Grammar School course, in the schools in which the study of said language may be introduced; and whenever said course shall be pursued, such additional time shall be given to each grade as may be required to enable the pupils thoroughly to complete the progress prescribed for that grade.

SEVENTH AND EIGHTH GRADES.

The *alphabet*, both printed and script, with simple exercises in reading and writing, by dictation and by copying.

Oral translation of simple sentences in German and English, including subjects and predicates of various forms, with instruction in the use of the *article*, and the *present tense* of *regular verbs*, and of the verb *sein*.

Colloquial exercises in the same.

SIXTH GRADE.

Reading and *writing*, by dictation and copying, continued; *oral* and *written translation* of simple sentences, in German and English, including subject, predicate, object and simple adjuncts, with instruction in the *gender*, *number*, and *case* of *nouns* and *pronouns*, the present and past tenses of regular verbs, and of the verbs *sein* and *haben.*

Colloquial exercises by the use of similiar sentences.

FIFTH GRADE.

Reading and *writing* continued, as in the preceding grades.

Oral and written translation of simple sentences in German and English, including phrases and the use of the preposition; also of easy compound sentences, with instruction in the declension and comparison of adjectives, the declension of pronouns, and the conjugation of the indicative mood of regular verbs, and of the verbs *sein* and *haben.*

Colloquial exercises, adapted to the progress of the pupil.

FOURTH GRADE.

Reading and *writing* continued, as before.

Oral and *written translation* of simple and compound sentences in English and German, affording practice in the case of nouns and pronouns, the tenses of the indicative and imperative moods of regular verbs in both voices, and the use of adjectives and adverbs, with instruction in grammar, as applicable to such sentences.

Colloquial exercises on the same.

THIRD GRADE.

Reading from a German reader, with translation into English; *writing,* by copying and dictation.

Oral and *written translation* of sentences, in German and English, affording practice in the regular and irregular verbs (indicative mood), with instruction in grammar continued.

Colloquial exercises.

SECOND GRADE.

Reading and *translation* from the German Reader continued; *memorizing* and *recitation* of select passages; *writing,* by dictation and copying, continued; *oral* and *written translation* of sentences, in German and English, affording practice in the indicative and subjunctive moods of regular and irregular verbs; *grammar* continued; German composition commenced.

Colloquial exercises in all the topics of the previous grades.

FIRST GRADE.

Reading and *translation* of select passages; elocution, *oral* and *written translation* of miscellaneous passages in German and English; the *Grammar* completed and reviewed; *German composition* continued, including epistolary and business forms.

Colloquial exercises and conversations on promiscuous topics.

Whenever the study of German shall have been introduced as above, it shall be pursued in the several grades according to the course of instruction prescribed by the Board; and pupils shall be required to show the proficiency assigned to each grade before being promoted to a higher grade (By-Laws, § 84).

GENERAL REGULATIONS RELATIVE TO INSTRUCTIONS IN THE SEVERAL GRADES OF THE GRAMMAR SCHOOL COURSE.

Lessons and Recitations.—(By-Laws, § 79.) "No lesson shall be given to a pupil to be learned out of school until it shall have been sufficiently explained and illustrated by the teacher to the class; nor shall the lessons be such as to require a period of study each day, in the case of a child of ordinary capacity, longer than two hours. Exercises in grammatical analysis and parsing, and written and mental arithmetic, shall not be assigned for home study, except to pupils of the first grade."

1. In every class, however well graded, the pupils will differ much in age, health, mental capacity, and home advantages. A correct and judicious classification by the principal will reduce this inequality to a minimum; but there will still remain a wide field for the exercise of discrimination, care, and caution on the part of the class teacher. The lessons should, in all respects, be adapted to the average ability of the pupils of the class; but, even beyond this, some allowance will often have to be made in the case of pupils of quite inferior mental capacity or opportunities for home study. Teachers must bear in mind that the one great object of home study is to train the pupils to self-exertion,—to give them the ability to depend upon their own efforts as students, and by degrees, to dispense with the aid of a teacher. It is, therefore, of supreme importance to avoid everything that would discourage, or deprive of self-reliance; and nothing has a stronger tendency in this direction than the imposition of excessive tasks.

2. Teachers are especially admonished to be considerate toward pupils of a delicate constitution, an over-excitable brain and nervous system, or in temporary ill-health. Many children of this class are precocious in mental activity and exceedingly ambitious to excel; and the greatest care is required to prevent them from injuring themselves by an inordinate devotion to books and study.

3. The *length* of the tasks imposed should be most carefully scrutinized and adjusted. The practice of assigning a *fixed number* of words, lines, paragraphs, pages, or examples, without a minute inspection of their nature or contents, is often accompanied with disastrous results. The pupils are wearied and discouraged; and the parents, finding the work of the school-room transferred to the home-circle, lose all confidence in the judgment and ability of the teacher.

4. The teacher should ascertain the methods which pupils employ in home-study. Verbatim study, excepting in case of important definitions, is to be discouraged. While making the necessary preliminary explanations, a brief abstract of the leading points should be written upon the blackboard, and made the basis of the recitation. This will do much to induce a rational method in study, and prevent a slavish adherence to the text.

5. Unless thoroughly familiar with the details of the text-book, the teacher needs special and renewed preparation quite as much as the pupils. Without this, he will not succeed. In hearing the recitation, he should carefully discriminate between the statements found in the text-book and those additional ones which he may have found necessary to make in the preparatory explanation of the lesson, and which the pupil may have had no opportunity to con over.

6. The recitations should be spirited exercises. The questions should be as definite as possible. The teacher should carefully avoid stating in the question any of those facts or principles that should be given by the pupil. The habit of

repeating the pupil's answer should also be avoided. Pupils should be invariably required to use natural and proper tones in recitation, to enunciate distinctly, and to avoid errors in speech. If this be not done, the special lessons of the reading-book or the grammar will be of little avail to break up the pernicious habits of speech which the teacher has himself, by his neglect, assisted to fix.

7. The teacher should advise with his pupils as to their hours and opportunities for home-study. Household duties, cramped and noisy homes, and bad light, no doubt greatly interfere in many cases. These should be as far as possible ascertained and allowed for. Very small print should be entirely excluded from home-lessons on account of its tendency to produce myopie when studied by artificial light. The many hours of confinement in the crowded class-room, and the long-continued and close attention required there, make mental rest and relaxation, with some kind of physical exercise, indispensable to growing boys and girls. The teacher should advise that these come before home-study.

Reviews.—(By-Laws, § 80.) "On the last Friday of each month, there shall be, in every class, a general review of all the studies of the previous month, at which review all text-books shall be laid aside by teachers and pupils."

Exhibitions.—(By-Laws, § 80.) "No public exhibition requiring special preparation shall be given in any school or department (Primary or Grammar), if at all, oftener than once during each year, except by permission of the Board of Trustees."

Physical Training.—The pupils should be exercised as much as is practicable in such a way as to expand the lungs, develop the muscular system, and impart an easy and graceful carriage to the body. In the Boys' Grammar Schools, the marching drill should be employed in the ordinary evolutions of the schools, the pupils receiving such instruction as may be required to make it effective. Light gymnastic and calisthenic exercises should be employed as far as may be requisite or suitable for the general objects of physical training, or a profitable relaxation after the severer mental exercises.

Manners and Morals.—(See page 54.) The directions given in relation to Primary Schools are equally applicable to Grammar Schools, and should receive a proper degree of attention.

Promotion from Primary to Grammar Schools.—(By-Laws, § 76.) "Promotions shall be made from the Primary to the Grammar Schools, semi-annually, and not oftener, except by the written permission of the City Superintendent; and no pupils shall be promoted from any Primary School, unless examined in all the studies prescribed for the First Grade of the Course of Instruction for Primary Schools, and found qualified by the Principal of the Department into which the promotion is to be made; and when so found qualified, such pupils shall be promoted without delay. Pupils may be transferred from the Primary to the Grammar Schools before completing the First Primary School Grade, with the consent of the Committee on Course of Study, School Books, and Hygienics, and on the recommendation of the City Superintendent, to whom application may be made by the Trustees in any ward, showing that said transfer is necessary in order to relieve the crowded condition of any Primary School, and to supply vacancies in the classes of the Grammar Schools. Pupils thus transferred to any Grammar School shall, however, be taught in the Primary Grade until regularly promoted from the same, but may be counted as a part of the regular attendance of the Grammar School."

Suspension of Incorrigible Pupils.—(By-Laws, § 40.) "Any pupil found to be incorrigible, or persistently disobedient to, and regardless of, the rules and regulations prescribed for the government of the school or class, or of resisting the authority of the Principal or class-teacher, or who, by a reckless depravity, may injure or demoralize the school or class, may be suspended by the Principal from the school. It shall be the duty of the Principal of every school thus suspending a pupil to give immediate notice thereof to the parents or guardian of such pupil, and also to report the same to the City Superintendent and to the Chairman of the Board of Trustees of the ward."

Duties of Teachers.—(By-Laws, § 38.) "It shall be the duty of every teacher to occupy the whole of each school session, or time for which the teacher is employed, in the purposes of instruction, or the making of entries necessary to be made at the time."

This By-Law applies to all teachers, whether employed in Primary or Grammar Schools.

Review of Preceding Studies (By-Laws, § 78.) " Every examination for promotion to a higher grade shall be preceded by a thorough review of all the studies pursued in the grade from which said promotion is to be made."

www.ingramcontent.com/pod-product-compliance
Lightning Source LLC
LaVergne TN
LVHW021400110826
845150LV00007B/1729

9781425512675